THE
NORTH CASCADES
NATIONAL
PARK

by Bob and Ira Spring
text by Harvey Manning

Superior PUBLISHING COMPANY

SEATTLE, WASH.

Picture Lake and Mt. Shuksan after an October snowfall.

LIBRARY OF CONGRESS NUMBER 77-80655

COPYRIGHT CANADA 1969

By

SUPERIOR PUBLISHING COMPANY

ALL RIGHTS RESERVED

FIRST EDITION

Printed and bound in Canada by Evergreen Press, Limited, Vancouver

Dedicated to Senator Henry M. Jackson,
Congressmen Lloyd Meeds, Thomas M. Pelly, and Thomas Foley,
and the thousands of Americans
who labored long and successfully
to create the North Cascades National Park

When President Lyndon B. Johnson signed the North Cascades legislation he also turned from the first to the second chapter of the North Cascades National Park. The first chapter, almost 60 years in length, started with the initial park proposal of 1906. It ended in 1968 with creation of the national park, finally considered by Congress to be politically expedient, though in our opinion the result is far less than optimum.

Early in the second chapter the necessity of enlarging the Park, Wilderness, and Recreation Areas to their ecologically optimum sizes is recognized. This chapter, however, largely unwritten and of uncertain length, will be subject to many revisions before it is finished. In it conservationists will be described as tirelessly seeking to add the critical forested corridor approaches to the scenic heartland of the region. These are the valleys that conservationists initially proposed for park or wilderness protection but which were excluded because others believed their forests were destined to be logged. This is the compromise that Congress presented to President Johnson and it is the compromise which conservationists shall seek to correct with the following additions:

More of the Cascade River valley should be added to the park. Only the upper six miles of the North Fork, below Cascade Pass, have been included. The five miles of existing roadside in this too-short section of a major entrance valley will almost immediately become overcrowded. By moving the

Coleman Glacier on Mt. Baker.

boundary westward, living space could be quadrupled in this only west-side valley containing adequate potential park campsites. The entire Cascade River drainage upstream from Marble Creek (except for portions already within the Glacier Peak Wilderness Area) should be included in the park. Ten additional miles of existing road in a lowland forested valley would thus be added, providing one of the park's most scenic entrances. This would place within the park and Glacier Park Wilderness Area all of the Cascade River drainage included by conservationists in their 1963 proposal for a national park.

The entire Granite Creek valley should be added to the park. While the North Cascades Study Team Report (by Agriculture and Interior representatives, 1966) described this valley as one where "there is no question as to the physical qualifications of the area for park status," it was not included in the North Cascades National Park or Ross Lake National Recreation Area. Instead, it has been left exposed to Forest Service multiple-use practices. The route of the North Cross-State Highway, the logical major visitor-access road, runs the length of this valley. As much of this highway as possible should be placed within the park to afford its forest environment and alpine scenic climax at Washington Pass the very highest form of scenic protection. Park Service interpretive facilities could thus be located along the highway and Granite Creek valley would also provide much-needed living space within the park, thereby relieving pressures to build additional roads into national park wilderness.

The Mt. Baker region should be added to enlarge the park,

as proposed by the National Park Service in the North Cascades Study Team report. Here is the only sector of the entire Cascade Range that illustrates all chapters of its geological story. Mt. Baker and its immediate vicinity provide a record upon which a complete story of the Cascade Range can be illustrated and interpreted. This is the best location—unique to this particular portion of the North Cascades—to witness conclusive geologic proof that long before the present Cascade Range was formed, a succession of great mountain ranges ancestral to the range of today existed. Beneath Mt. Baker's base, the very young volcanic deposits of the peak are in direct contact with the very old eroded surfaces of the ancestral mountains.

Major alleviation of the grossly inadequate park visitation provisions could be provided for at the already developed Heather Meadow area between Mt. Baker and Mt. Shuksan. The existing ski installations here could continue as structures predating the park, and need not serve as a precedent for the construction of additional facilities elsewhere within the park.

Sulphur, Downey, and Buck Creeks of the Suiattle River drainage should be added, each in its entirety, to the Glacier Peak Wilderness Area. One mile of Sulphur Creek, two miles of Downey Creek, and five miles of Buck Creek are still unprotected from logging. These are *de facto* wilderness valleys, logically part of the Glacier Peak Wilderness wherein their headwaters lie. They are lowland valleys leading into the heart of one of the most heavily glacier-clad regions of the Cascade Crest: the Snowking, Buckindy, Dome Peak, Ptarmigan Traverse section, between Cascade Pass and Image Lake. These valleys were deliberately excluded by the Forest Service because there are "too many commercial trees there."

The White Chuck valley eastward 1.5 miles from the present road-end should be added to the Glacier Peak Wilderness Area. This valley is the classic lowland wilderness walk in the western Cascades. It is only five miles by easy trail to the Kennedy Hot Springs camp at the western base of Glacier Peak. This is the most heavily used wilderness trail in the Mt. Baker National Forest; every possible mile of it must be kept as is for the easy wilderness experience it affords.

The Forest Service's Meadow Mountain timber sale of 1961, in the White Chuck valley, is a classic example of insensitivity to superb scenic values. This sale crystallized conservationists' recognition of the need for the scenic core of the North Cascades to be placed under the maximum protection of the National Park Service.

The eastern slopes above Lake Chelan, for 20 miles down to Safety Harbor Creek, should be added to the Lake Chelan National Recreation Area. As one travels up Lake Chelan, the mountain scenery starts suddenly and dramatically at Safety Harbor Creek. Also to this recreation area should be added the corresponding western slopes above Lake Chelan, together with the ten-to-fifteen miles of the Entiat and Chiwawa River drainages immediately south of the Glacier Peak Wilderness Area. Due to the extensive hunting recreation pattern established here a Lake Chelan National Mountain Recreation Area was proposed by the North Cascades Conservation Council in 1963.

The Glacier Peak-Image Lake region of the Glacier Peak Wilderness Area is one of the most scenic in the entire Cascades. The Kennecott Copper Corporation plans an open-pit mine in the very heart of this area, within a mile of Image Lake. Plans call for constructing roads to the mine, operating a mill and dumping waste tailings for 20 to 30 years — all within the Wilderness Area. Transfer of this region from Forest Service to Park Service administration would place greater restrictions on mining operations, permit condemnation and purchase of patented mining claims, and eliminate further prospecting. The North Cascades Conservation Council's 1963 park proposal, which included this region as the wilderness core, would provide much-increased protection for this scenically superlative terrain. Eventually the Glacier Peak Wilderness Area together with adjacent portions of the Suiattle, White Chuck, Sauk, Stillaguamish, Little Wenatchee, White, and Chiwawa River drainages should be added to the North Cascades National Park.

The final chapter, also unwritten, is one wherein protection in perpetuity will be provided for the North Cascades National Park, the Glacier Peak and Pasayten Wilderness Areas, and the Ross Lake and Lake Chelan National Recreation Areas.

Patrick Donovan Goldsworthy, President
North Cascades Conservation Council

Air view of Mt. Redoubt and the Redoubt Glacier; in distance at left, Shuksan and Baker.

When work on this book began, early in 1968, many of us felt we were 5 years away from our long-sought goal of a North Cascades National Park. Now as I write these words one of the famous years in the conservation history of the North Cascades — and the nation — is receding in memory, shaping into legend.

I remember hiking last March through forests on the snow-covered Cascade River road with the Boy, 4, and Youngest Daughter, 8, to close under Cascade Pass, avalanches sloughing off the mile-high wall of Johannesberg, sunlight flaring between gray-black clouds, and wondering what sort of nation it was that had not long since placed this valley within one of America's finest National Parks. By then the park bill had passed the Senate, but the Interior Committee of the House of Representatives, tyrannized by a man whose intellectual growth ended with the 19th century, was expected to bury the legislation deep.

Though semi-despairing, what a greeting we gave the Committee when it visited Seattle last spring! By the hundreds the faithful crowded the hearing rooms, in mood and demeanor somewhere between an anti-war rally and a lynch mob. Congressmen who came to Seattle sympathetic were gratified, those who came neutral were impressed, those who came hostile left on the bandwagon — or so they said.

Summer was a time of anticipation and tension. All the grand week the Manning Gang plus Ira roamed high meadows of Copper Mountain, across the Chilliwack valley from the Pickets, I kept thinking (crossing fingers) that on our next visit here this would be *park*. When Ted Beck, Dick Brooks, Pat Goldsworthy, and I hiked from Ross Lake through forests of Little Beaver and Big Beaver Creeks, with an off-trail side-trip to Luna Cirque, we visually fondled old, old cedars, rivers, beaver marshes, and hanging glaciers which soon (cross fingers) would receive the honor — and more important, the protection — deserved.

But mysterious things were happening in Washington D.C. and it began to seem the powerful "hostiles" on the House Interior Committee had said encouraging words only to escape Seattle un-hung. Waiting, living from rumor to rumor, July and August were a succession of hopes and glooms. Then September and our friends in Congress defeated last-gasp machinations and the House passed the bill and on October 2 President Johnson signed the North Cascades Act and suddenly we had the park — and blinked with amazement, recalling that 5 months earlier we'd been resigned to another 5 years in the trenches.

The fall dinner meeting of the North Cascades Conservation Council was as wild as the park we were gathered to celebrate; from postcards and letters I know other members were assembled in smaller groups all across the country, trying to uncross their fingers.

The celebrations are over. Now, time to begin the next campaign. Because the 1968 North Cascades Act is more important for the *recognition* it gives than for the *protection*.

Indeed, were preservationists to relax, thinking the job done, the 1968 Act could be the instrument for accelerating the destruction of wildlands; its passage is being cited in some quarters as an excuse for stepping up the exploitation of *de facto* wilderness in National Forests bordering the park.

The purpose of this book is to encourage Americans to come from everywhere to enjoy their North Cascades National Park, and their Ross Lake and Lake Chelan National Recreation Areas, and their Glacier Peak and Pasayten Wilderness Areas, and also the portions of their North Cascades which deserve but lack protected status. The New Campaign, which begins now, must enroll more recruits. The Old Campaign mainly saved non-controversial lands — trees uneconomic to log, rocks lacking valuable minerals, a game population too small for any considerable hunting, meadows and glaciers good only for walking and admiring. Even so the logging lobby, the mining lobby, the hunting lobby, and even the mechanized skiing lobby (despite a lack of terrain suitable for commercial development) fought bitterly and tenaciously. Why? Principally, I think, because though the North Cascades Act took away from them little they valued, they realized its passage would put the area in a national spotlight and pose a future threat to their special greeds.

If the exploiters fought before, what will they do now, as the New Campaign seeks to save lands that *are* controversial?

So, this book is intended as an invitation to come enjoy — and then help save.

There is much to enjoy that can be enjoyed easily, by anyone; in following pages the "Introduction to the North Cascades" lists guidebooks that tell how to drive to virgin forests, highland meadows, close views of glaciers and peaks, and how to penetrate the wilderness fringes and center on short walks and long.

However, after reading my stories Ira has seriously questioned whether I am extending an invitation to roam — or trying to reduce population pressure by scaring people away. Sure enough, many of the described trips involve wicked bugs and horrid storms and thirst and exhaustion and fear. ("This is an *invitation?*" asks Ira.)

Well, wilderness is wild. Sometimes it isn't nice. Sometimes it frightens little children, not to mention grown men.

Suffering is not indispensable to a North Cascades experience, and my family and I have spent countless days there sniffing flowers and feeling no pain. But the essence of wilderness is: no guarantees.

Though the fringes are friendly, the heart of the North Cascades is no-guarantee wilderness and so it must remain.

In writing this book — this recruiting brochure — I have told how it really is in the North Cascades, as the Manning Gang and friends have known it. Not all flowers and sunshine. If it were we wouldn't be so intrigued.

Harvey Manning
Cougar Mountain
January, 1969

One: Glacier Peak

(See Chapter 1, "One Waterfall Camp".)

The last wild volcano, the only one in the Washington Cascades without roads on its flanks, lies deep in the range. Until recently Glacier was the volcano nobody knew; most citizens of Seattle still confuse it with Mt. Baker and when in a position to see both peaks on the horizon are confused and baffled.

Glacier's 10,528-foot elevation dominates without overpowering mountains famous in their own right among climbers and hikers. The presence can never be ignored. Even when the peak cannot be seen, one may be walking through pumice deposited by the eruption of 12,000 years ago, an instant in geologic time.

The volcano slopes, the glacier rock milk, fall into west-side valleys. Surrounding peaks, many above 8,000 feet, drain snow waters not only west but east.

Two: Lake Chelan

(See Chapter 2, "Prince Creek".)

The 55-mile-long lake, never much more than a mile wide, occupying a trench gouged by a Pleistocene glacier, rules its province as surely as any volcano, though more subtly. The lake surface, 1,000 feet above sealevel under steep slopes with unbroken rises of 6,000 feet and more, can be seen only from nearby, but in all directions alpine travelers "feel" the gulf dividing the Cascade Crest from the Chelan Crest.

Country west of the lake is in the rainshadow of the Cascade Crest and thus less snowy and cloudy than the Glacier vicinity. Elevations and dimensions are impressive, culminating in 9,511-foot Bonanza, highest non-volcanic peak in Washington.

The Chelan Crest east of the lake has summits to 8,400 feet, but the terrain is rounded, nibbled rather than chomped by ancient ice. High, rolling meadows at 6,500-7,500 feet melt free of snow in late June, a month earlier than the main range. Few of the summer storms that bring drizzle and fog to windward slopes send more than empty clouds here. From the "sunshine mountains" one looks west over the Chelan trench to white giants of the Cascade Crest, east over heat-shimmering brown hills across the Methow River.

The Stehekin River, a master stream of the North Cascades, enters the lake head. With tributaries flowing from 9,000-foot peaks along miles of the Cascade Crest, with no road access from "outside", the Stehekin is one of America's genuinely wild rivers. As a geographical unit, Lake Chelan and the Stehekin are without comparison in all the mountains of the nation.

Three: Ptarmigan Traverse

(See Chapter 3, "White Rock Lakes".)

North of Glacier Peak the Cascade Crest rises to the Ptarmigan Traverse, so called for the pioneering 1938 high-line tour by four young members of the Ptarmigan Climbing Club. In the 30 miles from Suiattle Pass to Cascade Pass, no trail ever has been built to the cold and rugged Crest (and may none ever be built). The south end of the line is anchored by 8,860-foot Dome Peak with its large glaciers and sharp satellites, the north end by Johannesberg and Magic; between lies a wildland of

NATURE'S PLAN

To the west, saltwater straits and bays. Green lowlands. Moist maritime air. The Puget Sound Basin.

To the east, golden hills and lava plateaus. Sunshine in the semi-arid rainshadow. The Columbia Basin.

The range, narrow in the south, here bulges wide, merging east into the Okanogan Highlands (and thus the Rockies), merging north into the British Columbia Coast Range (and thus the Yukon and Alaska).

A pair of volcanoes more than 2 miles high, streaming white ice. Other tall peaks by the hundreds, other broad glaciers.

A pair of freshwater fjords, deep lakes many miles long amid steep-walled mountains, water roads to wilderness.

Forests and rivers of windward valleys, entryways from cool tidewater. And forests and rivers of leeward valleys, draining snow-melt to sagebrush.

Trees and flowers, waterfalls and icefalls, gorges and cliffs, horns for climbing and ridges for running.

The master plan by which these elements are organized into the North Cascades is complex, and any geographical description must either be encyclopedic or over-simplified. In following pages seven rather approximate "mountain provinces" are described; they could as well be broken into smaller units or combined into quite different provinces. However, they'll do for an introduction.

Thunder Arm of Diablo Lake, Colonial Peak above.

ice and cliff only the experienced alpine traveler can enter. However, trails approach the Crest close enough for hikers to gain near views.

The valleys are important. Too much can be said, and perhaps has been said, about glaciers, rocks, and meadows. Antarctica and Greenland and Alaska have far more massive glaciers, and the world is full of rocks, and Iceland and northern Canada, Alaska, and the Soviet Union are a vastness of meadows.

What gives these glaciers, rocks, and meadows their special quality — what gives the range its distinctive character — are the virgin forests in valleys draining west to Puget Sound and east to Lake Chelan and the Columbia River. Even if the highest summits of the North Cascades were low and rounded, the forests would be a masterwork in America's gallery of natural treasures.

To sit beside a loud, cold river amid mosses and ferns under a Douglas fir 400 years old and glimpse ice hanging far above on the walls of a spire — this is the North Cascades.

Four: Eldorado to Silver Star

(See Chapter 4, "Many Waterfalls Camp".)
North of Cascade Pass the range is so broad and varied one could distinguish several distinct provinces. However, the immensity and diversity make a unity of sorts.

The south boundary is the Cascade River-Stehekin River line; the north, the route of the North Cross-State Highway under construction along the Skagit River, Ruby Creek, Granite Creek, Rainy Pass, Washington Pass, and Early Winters Creek. On the west are 8,868-foot Eldorado and 8,347-foot Snowfield, on the east 8,876-foot Silver Star. These are only a few of the high summits; many of the grandest peaks and largest glaciers in the Cascades are here.

And splendid valleys, too, windward and leeward both. The green-misty luxury of west-side forests has been noted. But to sprawl in sunshine on dry grass beneath a Ponderosa pine and look up to ice and to melting-away cloud scraps — this, too, is the North Cascades.

Five: Baker and Shuksan

(See Chapter 5, "The Great Shuksan Fiasco".)
Mt. Baker, rising 10,750 feet above saltwater 30 miles distant, is a familiar landmark around Puget Sound. Winter storms sweeping inland from the ocean hit Baker first, dumping skyfuls of snow that often accumulate to depths of 20 feet; from every side the mountain appears to be a virtually solid mass of glaciers.

Facing the white volcano across forests of Swift Creek is 9,127-foot Shuksan, a classic of mountain architecture. The two peaks are a magnificent pair, unmatched in all America. Meadow ridges allow easy-walking close-up enjoyment of both.

Six: The Pickets

(See Chapter 6, "Luna Cirque".)
The Pickets are the climax of Cascades rough-and-tough wildness—as if the range, which ends close by in Canada, saved its best effort for the last. Even now the interior has been walked by mere hundreds of travelers, and until recently the very name was unknown except to climbers. But the word has gotten out and the Pickets have become abruptly famous.

On the west are small mountains and meadow basins — and also the Border Peaks, dominated by the terrible tower of Slesse. In the core are the Southern Pickets, or Terror Group; the Northern Pickets, or Fury Group; and the Chilliwacks, or Redoubt Group. East is the Skagit River, now drowned by Ross Lake, a reservoir that (when brimful) is a fit companion for Lake Chelan.

Seven: The Wild, Wild East

(See Chapter 7, "Running the Eastern Ridges".)
East of Ross Lake is the largest and lonesomest province of the range.

One sub-province is between Ross Lake and the Cascade Crest, with peaks as high and mighty as 8,928-foot Jack and dozens of others at 8,000 feet or near; but also, amid sculpted summits and bits of ice and torrents roaring in canyons, a glory of ridges built for flower-roaming.

The other sub-province extends east from the Crest to the Okanogan Highlands, doubly or triply rainshadowed, with good weather and relatively gentle profile. All summits are walks or scrambles, even the many that rise above 8,000 feet. Meadows are on a huge scale; forested valleys, too. The few travelers of the present are swallowed in immensity.

Long after solitude is hard to find in the Pickets, there'll be quiet corners here.

MAN'S PLAN

In the late 19th and early 20th centuries, portions of the American West were exempted from terms of the Homestead Act and similar frontier legislation designed to transfer empty public land as swiftly as possible into private ownership. Called "Forest Reserves" and then "National Forests", they were — and are — maintained as property of the entire nation (*not* merely the adjacent residents) by the U.S. Forest Service, an agency of the Department of Agriculture. Except for a few homesteads predating the Reserves, and a scattering of tracts taken from the public domain under the Mining Laws of 1872 (the only frontier-era land law that continues in force to this day — a scandal that must be dealt with soon to avoid wildland disasters), the entire interior of the North Cascades is publicly owned.

Also in the late 19th century the first National Parks were established. In 1916 the National Park Service was created as an agency of the Department of the Interior, charged to preserve the parks as "museums of primitive America". With the North Cascades Act signed into law by President Lyndon B. Johnson on October 2, 1968, the Park Service entered the North Cascades, taking over certain lands (see below) from the Forest Service.

The 1968 legislation has a notable and unparalleled aspect: Congress specifically stated its intent that the Forest Service and Park Service should co-ordinate their planning and management to treat the North Cascades as a single unit; this strongly specific statement can only be the result of the long and unswerving (and unfinished) campaign by private citizens banded together in preservation groups, led by the North Cascades Conservation Council, to gain maximum possible protection for *all* the North Cascades. Whether the intent of Congress will be carried out remains to be seen: the Forest

Service vigorously resisted loss of jurisdiction to the Park Service; only time will tell whether it will take special care of lands adjacent to the new National Park, thus saving proper entries to the Park, or resume its subtle bureaucratic war and force preservationists to seek, once more, recourse to Congress.

The Wilderness Act of 1964 also has major significance for the North Cascades. Under its terms any federal lands, in National Forests or National Parks or other jurisdictions, may be placed by Congress in the National Wilderness Preservation System, where "the earth and its community of life are un-trammeled by man, where man himself is a visitor who does not remain." As discussed below, much of the North Cascades is included in the system and more soon will be.

These two federal agencies manage the North Cascades in a variety of categories. Following is a survey of "man's plan" as it now stands. (The roles of other governmental agencies are omitted here, but it should be noted the "plan" also involves the federal Bureau of Public Roads, the Washington State Game Department and Highways Department, Seattle City Light, and additional federal, state, municipal, and private-enterprise groups.)

U.S. Forest Service

The North Cascades contain all or part of four National Forests: Mt. Baker (all), Wenatchee (all), Okanogan (part), and Snoqualmie (part).

The Multiple Use Act of 1960 gave force of law to the long-existing philosophy of the Forest Service, which is to manage lands for "multiple-use" — that is, simultaneously to extract a number of commodities from the same area. For example, in an ideal (from the Forest Service view) multiple-use valley, logging, mining, and hydroelectric developments are conducted along with fishing, hunting, skiing, camping, horse-riding, motorcycle-riding, hiking, and every other conceivable commercial and recreational activity. Unfortunately, the slogan often leads to "multiple-abuse," since some uses are obviously

(except to the Forest Service) incompatible; fishing and water-skiing don't mix well on a lake, nor hiking and motorcycling on a trail, nor logging and botanizing in a forest, nor goat-watching and goat-shooting on a peak, and so on.

Under public pressure the Forest Service sometimes reluctantly retreats from full-scale multiple-use. A few trails have been closed to motorized vehicles and even to horses. Some areas of heavy recreational use have been designated "land-scape management areas", meaning the logging proceeds a bit slower than usual and the scars are somewhat screened by trees left standing along roads and trails.

In general, though, any portion of a National Forest not given specific protection is open to multiple-use — and multiple-abuse. Following are the major units which presently have specific protection.

Glacier Peak Wilderness Area

The Glacier Peak Wilderness Area of 458,500 acres was set aside in 1960 by administrative action of the Forest Service; in 1964 it was included by Congress in the National Wilderness Preservation System.

Preservationists had been working for years before 1960 to gain wilderness status for the Glacier Peak region. Upon seeing the Forest Service plan, they denounced it as "wilderness on the rocks", a "starfish" of rocky ridges radiating from glaciers at the center, excluding every valley with significant quantities of trees worth logging. Preservationist protests caused the Secretary of Agriculture to partially over-rule the Forest Service by adding forests of the Suiattle River and Agnes Creek. However, the result was still inadequate, and this gross example of Forest Service insensitivity led directly to the renewed and at last successful movement for a National Park.

Ironically, the park as finally created omits Glacier Peak. The 1968 legislation did add 10,000 acres to the Glacier Peak Wilderness Area in Downey Creek, Sulphur Creek, Suiattle River,

Sauk River valley.

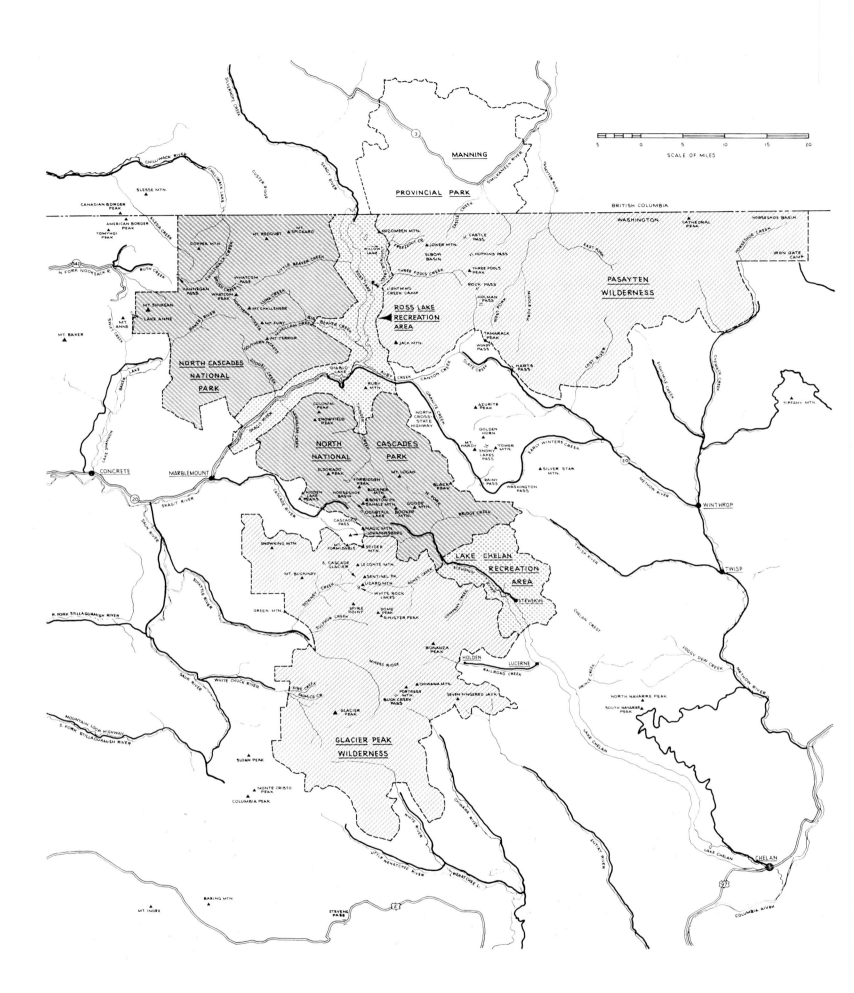

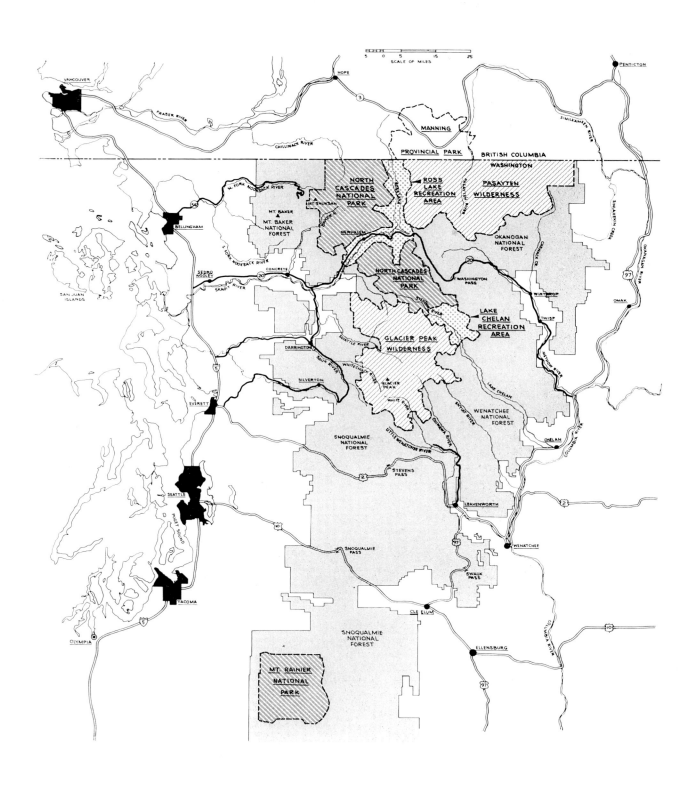

SCALE OF MILES

VANCOUVER
HOPE
PENTICTON

FRASER RIVER

CHILLIWACK RIVER

SIMILKAMEEN RIVER

MANNING

PROVINCIAL PARK   BRITISH COLUMBIA
                         WASHINGTON

NORTH
CASCADES
NATIONAL
PARK

ROSS
LAKE
RECREATION
AREA

PASAYTEN
WILDERNESS

M. FORK NOOKSACK RIVER

MT. BAKER

BELLINGHAM

MT. BAKER
NATIONAL
FOREST

MT. SHUKSAN

OKANOGAN
NATIONAL
FOREST

S. FORK NOOKSACK RIVER

SEDRO
WOOLEY

CONCRETE

NORTH CASCADES
NATIONAL
PARK

SAN JUAN
ISLANDS

SKAGIT RIVER

WASHINGTON PASS

WINTHROP

OMAK

LAKE
CHELAN
RECREATION
AREA

TWISP

SUIATTLE RIVER

GLACIER PEAK
WILDERNESS

DARRINGTON

SAUK RIVER

WHITECHUCK RIVER

SILVERTON

GLACIER PEAK

LAKE CHELAN

EVERETT

WHITE RIVER

CHIWAWA RIVER

WENATCHEE
NATIONAL
FOREST

SEATTLE

CHELAN

COLUMBIA RIVER

SNOQUALMIE
NATIONAL
FOREST

LITTLE WENATCHEE RIVER

PUGET SOUND

STEVENS
PASS

LEAVENWORTH

WENATCHEE

TACOMA

SNOQUALMIE
PASS

SWAUK
PASS

OLYMPIA

CLE ELUM

ELLENSBURG

SNOQUALMIE
NATIONAL
FOREST

MT. RAINIER
NATIONAL
PARK

COLUMBIA RIVER

and White Chuck River — not enough, leaving vulnerable much beautiful forest in the scenic heartland.

Unfortunately, the 1964 Wilderness Act, though barring logging, roads, and mechanized equipment, *allows mining* — a major and potentially fatal flaw. Kennecott Copper Corporation owns property in the wilderness core and unless stopped will dig a monstrous open-pit mine there. The Forest Service is powerless to block this unspeakable desecration.

Pasayten Wilderness Area

The 1968 North Cascades Act established the 520,000-acre Pasayten Wilderness Area, which had had temporary protection since 1935 as part of the North Cascades Primitive Area.

This wildland was never a matter of much controversy; commodity values are so minute the Forest Service proposal was nearly identical to that of preservationists.

However, another flagrant flaw of the Wilderness Act is exemplified here — grazing by cattle and sheep is allowed, though how this blends with wilderness values only the Forest Service understands. Two of the supreme highlands of the Pasayten Wilderness Area are currently unusable by the discriminating recreationist for most of the summer — unless he enjoys sharing his camp and drinking water with cows and examining what's left of the flowers after sheep have eaten their fill. The grazing, moreover, has a long-term and perhaps permanent effect on the plant and animal life of the ecosystem.

Mt. Baker Recreation Area

Way back in the 1920s, when the idea of a National Park in the North Cascades first gained some popularity, the Forest Service recognized the scenery (and the possible threat to its empire) by establishing the Mt. Baker Park Division, later re-named the Mt. Baker Recreation Area, of some 70,000 acres.

Several things are wrong with the designation. For one, boundaries include ice, rock, and meadows but few trees — which currently are being stripped from slopes of Baker at an hysterical pace. For another, a Forest Service recreation area is not very restrictive; at least two logging sales have been held *within* the boundaries. And finally, in the once-heavenly alpine parks of Heather Meadows, the Forest Service has allowed a hellish conglomeration of developments, many of which could and should have gone elsewhere.

Mt. Baker is in fact unprotected — except for the glaciers, for which no commercial use has been found. Yet.

National Park Service

National Parks are "museums of primitive America". Logging, mining, and other resource extractions are barred; all forms of recreation compatible with a "museum" quality are allowed. For example, fishing yes but hunting no. Trail hiking yes but trail motorcycling no. Roads, campgrounds, and other tourist facilities yes — but only when they do not destroy the natural scene visitors come to enjoy.

Just as with National Forests, portions of National Parks may be placed in the National Wilderness Preservation System; since hunting and mining and grazing are forbidden, National Park wilderness is of a far higher order than that in National Forests.

The National Park Service also administers National Recreation Areas, a lower status than National Park; hunting is permitted, a greater degree of development, and limited resource extraction where compatible with recreation.

North Cascades National Park

The 504,500-acre North Cascades National Park created in 1968 has two units: the north section centered on the Pickets; the south section centered on the Eldorado-Logan axis.

Nearly the entire park is planned for inclusion in the National Wilderness Preservation System — as nature demands, since the park is mostly cliffs, glaciers, and gorges.

The only fault with the park is what's left out. Aside from Glacier Peak and Mt. Baker, the west-side entryways, including the Nooksack and Baker and Cascade Rivers, remain under Forest Service control — and precisely in these valleys the multiple-abuse has been particularly notorious.

Ross Lake National Recreation Area

Between the two units of the park and the Pasayten Wilderness Area is the new (1968) 105,000-acre Ross Lake National Recreation Area, planned for high-use recreation, including an aerial tram from the North Cross-State Highway to the summit of Ruby Mountain to provide an easy high overlook of the North Cascades.

Again, the principal fault is what's left out: the entirety of Granite Creek, Rainy Pass, Washington Pass, and Early Winters Creek — the route of the North Cross-State Highway, which should become the North Cascades Parkway. All this country, plus the Cascade Crest north to Harts Pass, deserves National Park or at least National Recreation Area protection.

Lake Chelan National Recreation Area

At the upper end of Lake Chelan and in the lower Stehekin River is the new (1968) 62,000-acre Lake Chelan National Recreation Area.

Once more, the area is too small. Both shores of Lake Chelan from Safety Harbor Creek, the Chelan Crest east of the lake, valleys and peaks between the lake and the Glacier Peak Wilderness Area, and country south of the Glacier Peak Wilderness Area deserve a better fate than the Forest Service has in mind.

GATEWAYS

The accompanying map shows major automobile entries to the North Cascades and the places they lead to, including valleys and peaks mentioned in these pages.

A number of books are available providing detailed information on driving, camping, and hiking; the following are recommended to any traveler planning a visit to the range.

Trips and Trails, 1: Family Camps, Short Hikes, and View Roads in the North Cascades and Olympics. Text by E. M. Sterling, photos by Bob and Ira Spring, maps by Marge Mueller. The Mountaineers. $4.95.

This is the basic book, describing automobile campgrounds, hikes of an hour or an afternoon suitable for any person of whatever age or strength, and things to see from main highways and side roads. More than 100 photographs show what the country is like. Text and maps tell how to get there.

100 Hikes in Western Washington. Photos by Bob and Ira Spring, maps by Marge Mueller. The Mountaineers. $4.95.

Hikes from a short day to a long week. About one-third are in the North Cascades. For each there is a photo, map, and text giving directions and describing terrain. The book is indispensable for those who come to the range planning to take day hikes or backpacks.

Routes and Rocks: Hiker's Guide to the North Cascades from Glacier Peak to Lake Chelan. By D. F. Crowder and R. W. Tabor. The Mountaineers. $5.00.

The definitive book on hiking the Glacier Peak region. Description of trails and off-trail high routes in and around the Glacier Peak Wilderness Area and Lake Chelan, with notes on geology. Many line drawings and sketch maps. In a back pocket are three quadrangle maps with route and camp information.

Hiker's Map to the North Cascades: Routes and Rocks in the Mt. Challenger Quadrangle. By Tabor and Crowder. The Mountaineers. $2.95.

Essential for hikers and climbers in the Pickets and Chilliwacks, core of the north section of the North Cascades National Park. The text (with drawings and photos and geologic notes) explains trails, camps, and off-trail high routes shown on a quadrangle map in a back pocket.

Northwest Ski Trails. Text by Ted Mueller, photos by Bob and Ira Spring, maps by Marge Mueller. The Mountaineers. $4.95.

A book for snowtime, describing developed ski areas and wildland ski tours, including some in the North Cascades. Photos show the white mountains.

Snowshoe Hikes in the Cascades and Olympics. By Gene Prater. The Mountaineers. $3.50.

Another book for snowtime. Text and maps tell how to web a way into winter hills. A number of the trips are in the North Cascades.

The North Cascades. Photos by Tom Miller. The Mountaineers. $10.00.

High-mountain photographs, 68 in all, taken from a climber's viewpoint and displayed on large pages. Superb insights of the Glacier Peak Wilderness Area and the North Cascades National Park.

The Wild Cascades: Forgotten Parkland. By Harvey Manning, lines from Theodore Roethke. Sierra Club. $20.00. Ballantine-Sierra paper edition, $3.95.

Many photographs in black and white and color. Impressionistic essays about the range and a detailed narrative of the campaign to create a North Cascades National Park.

Challenge of the North Cascades. By Fred Beckey. The Mountaineers. $6.95.

Stories of first ascents over a 30-year period by a famous explorer of the range's most difficult wilderness peaks. Many photos and maps.

Climber's Guide to the North Cascades. By Fred Beckey. The Mountaineers. Scheduled for publication in 1970.

The author wrote the original guide to the Cascades, published in 1949 and now out of print. His new guide will obviously be as important as the old, which became known as "Beckey's Bible".

Eldorado Peak from Cascade Pass.

Contents

Air view across the Boston Glacier to Mt. Buckner.

One Waterfall Camp

Our Cougar Mountain basecamp is 650 feet above the mean high tide of Puget Sound. Driving 2½ hours to the end of the White Chuck River road would raise us only to 2300. The meadows begin several thousand feet higher.

Penny and Becky, 11 and 10, were solid backpackers. The infant boy could be cached in lowlands. Betty was in crummy post-partum shape and despondent about leaving her baby and that was one problem. Another was 5-year-old Claudia; on the trail, stubby legs sprouting from overstuffed rucksack, she often was mistaken for a self-propelled pack. Another was the timid old sheep dog with the piebald eyes, Tasha, feeling poorly and no puppy anymore.

It's a long lift from the White Chuck to the flowers, but there's no arguing with a Puritan Father, formerly an Eagle Scout. Since my introduction to Glacier Peak on a summit ascent 16 years earlier I'd developed a fondness for this prime blend of ice and gardens and forests. A comfortable wilderness, perfect for a family. As for the long lift, there's no cheap way to Glacier; only an experiment would tell if the Girl Guides were able to pay the price.

At road-end Saturday morning, August 8, we unloaded the microbus and loaded our backs. Several miles of White Chuck forests had been motheaten since my last visit. The south-bank trail had been abandoned — to be made ready for whacking into south-bank trees, I gloomily suspected. The new trail

Glacier Peak from Pumice Peak, the cirque of One Waterfall Camp below to the right.

followed the north bank, the first mile paralleling clear-cut logging patches. At 11 a.m. we hoisted packs. The sky was dull white. The forecast was storm.

At Fire Creek we stopped for lunch. Loud water, tall trees, soft moss. But no sunrays penetrated forest dank. The white sky was darkening to gray. Tasha coughed and shivered.

The trail climbed a short, stiff bit onto a flat terrace, remnant of the sand and gravel that once filled the entire valley. Near the top the trail-cut exposed a layer of pumice fragments, ash, and chunks of andesite blown from the mountain in a hot cloud and welded as it fell, still hot and sticky, into "tuff." I explained. Claudia uneasily looked around for the unseen volcano that had committed the violence. Could the same thing happen again — maybe today?

The terrace forest was gorgeous, and the green understory, and the mossy old logs, but the trail was a drainage trench and the humus had been horse-churned into over-the-boots muck. The alternative was to walk beside the trail, beating through that fine green understory, stepping and scrambling over those mossy old logs. Party pace fell to less than a mile an hour.

At 4 p.m., Pumice Creek. Five hours and less than 4 miles. Still another long 2 miles to Kennedy Hot Springs, the next for-sure campsite. Afternoon was dooming-up, occasional splat-in-the-face drops filtering through the canopy. Time to establish wait-it-out Camp 1.

Rig tarp. The prospective bed of needles and humus squished and we lacked air mattresses or ensolite pads; fortunately, a winter-fallen tree provided fresh boughs for a dry sleep. In crannies we found combustible twigs. Pumice Creek was steps away; the frothy water was cold, cold.

Camp 1 was cold. Dark sky, saturated forest, stream breeze — and snowbanks. The winter had been rough and long, but snow at barely 3400 feet, in August? How summery would the high country be? With tarp and fire we could be comfortable by the river, in the trees, but how about upstairs?

Night rains came, rattling on the tarp, lullaby for a long

sleep. Morning tree-drips went pit-a-pat, pit-a-pat. Then rattle again. Lying in warm bags on soft boughs, we ate lunch for breakfast. Rain dwindled to mist, we crawled into gray noon, built fire, and had breakfast for lunch. Washed-out weekend hikers passed camp in a parade. The entire week lay ahead, but would my Girl Guides ever get out of the trees?

Camp lassitude was the danger. To keep legs loose and hope alive, in afternoon I herded the gang up-trail. Bad weather is good: the valley was empty, we had Kennedy Hot Springs to ourselves. Betty and I weren't tempted, not with fitful showers, clouds hanging in trees, river pounding close-by with a feeling of glaciers. Penny took the dare and when she survived Becky joined her but Claudia refused to descend the ladder into the steaming, bubbling, volcano-heated pool — a witch's cauldron if ever she saw one, the opaque yellow water full of who knows what, who knows whom.

Monday morning. Quiet tarp. Crawl out. Through the trees, blue sky. Even with snowbanks, even without sunrays, a warmth. The forest steamed. This was the day of the Push. Unrig camp and load backs and begin. Where oh where would we make Camp 2?

At the junction with the Kennedy Ridge trail, our route to the high country, a halt for lunch. Nobody was hungry, not at 11:30, an hour after breakfast, but here at 3300 feet was the last sure water until maybe 5500 feet. "Drink deep," I said. Nobody was thirsty, and some objected to the rock-milky water of Kennedy Creek. "Gives it body," said I, filling the poly bottle that would soon become the family's most precious possession. Now we had sunshine, and now we had heat. Shiver and drip, then swelter and sweat, that's the sport.

Switchbacks got directly to the business of leaving the valley. A step at a time, thoughts of the thousands of steps necessary before night. Some steps were shorter and slower and the party gradually separated. Tasha maintained liaison, now saying hello to Penny and me up front, then dashing back to check staggering Momma and friends, then leaping

Tasha cooling off after harrassing marmots.

and gasping to inspect the vanguard again; we worried that her frail health wasn't up to the responsibility.

Atop Kennedy Ridge the trail gentled out through big old trees along the crest. Amid forest we sensed vastness of valley below, mountain above. A sudden shock: a sign announcing the boundary of the Glacier Peak Wilderness Area. Penny cried, "But what about the *valley?*" Just 4 years earlier the Forest Service had established the Wilderness Area — leaving out, leaving for logging, all the forests through which we had walked. Penny, only 11, couldn't understand. Though much older, neither could I. (Nowadays, Forest Service officials act hurt and abused when we denounce them as enemies of the land. To which I say, "Remember the White Chuck!")

Through tree branches, looks down to alder jungles of Glacier Creek, glimpses of high whiteness. Onward into the Wilderness. The broad forest ridge narrowed to a light-timbered cat-walk with steep slopes falling left and right. Then a short drop from the cat-walk to a saddle and a junction with the Cascade Crest Trail, coming up Kennedy Creek. Tasha hadn't checked in for a long while — a bad sign. We rested, and rested more, until guilt sent us down-trail to pick up loads from suffering Momma and collapsing Claudia, only Becky holding her own. A re-grouping for second lunch and the last dregs from the canteen, haunted by sounds of distant creeks. If God is really good, why don't rivers flow closer to the ridges?

We were only halfway to highlands and the afternoon was shot. We'd never reach a decent camp by nightfall or exhaustion, whichever came first. I didn't say so, but my plot was to hike the Girl Guides until they dropped, then fetch enough water from somewhere for a survival camp at the point of collapse. Someday they'd thank me for all this, perhaps.

Tight switchbacks mounted a lava scarp, the brown-dusty cliffs dotted with tiny red strawberries — delicious, sweet, and damp. Time out for hunting red treasures hidden under leaves. An interlude of squealing joy amid misery past and misery to come.

Above strawberries the trail again followed a rounded crest — a moraine; geologically we now were *on* the mountain. Right, the deep trench of Kennedy Creek, braided channels of rock-milky water brawling from rock-milling ice. Left, Glacier Creek only a few hundred feet below, giving hope.

Penny and I again lost contact with the rearguard. Trees were shorter, alpine. Now heather — and heather is high country. Now patches of snow. Scoop handfuls to chew while walking. At a pinch we could cook supper with melted snow.

Late afternoon. Legs rubbery. Shoulders sagging under the stone. Shirt soaked with sweat. A thirst beyond what snow can quench. But Glacier Creek and the trail were converging. The waterfalls were energy.

Then the way swung off the moraine into a lush nook and a loud babble. Throw down packs and drink. Penny pulled off boots and dunked feet in a cold pool and screamed. I mixed a pot of purple punch and sprawled content, at home. I planned to start worrying about the rearguard, after a while. But propelled by strawberry-power, drawn by the sound of water, they straggled in — Tasha, Becky, and finally Betty and Claudia. The Girl Guides had conquered gravity. Few summits ever have given me such triumph as leading my troops to Camp 2.

Who could think our little high-country Glacier Creek, pouring between banks of grass and flowers, through groves of alpine fir, was the same Glacier Creek we'd crossed on a foot-log earlier the same day, down in big trees?

We got drunk on water and dirtied more water soaking feet. To make up for the pollution we gathered and buried 50 cans, 10 bottles, 5 pounds of aluminum foil, two frying pans, one pair of pants, and countless fragments of plastic tarps. Claudia tied a string to a stick and dangled it in the creek, fishing.

A short walk up the hillside to close views of Glacier Peak — we were on the volcano slopes. At sunset the icefalls glowed pink, the lava cliffs fire-red.

Avocados and lemon juice, heavily-salted cucumber slices, mushroom soup, Krap Dinner, pudding, tea — and bed. Most of the ground was either steep or snow-covered. The pooped rearguard sacked out on the only flat of any size and fell instantly asleep under stars; no need for a tarp in such weather, everything was going our way. Penny and I found a knoll big enough for two, the heather mattress a foot thick. But we didn't sleep.

A flash amid the fixed stars. Another. A long brightness with a misty aftertrail of eery dust. Another and another. The bombardment seemed threatening. We huddled close. Then a terrible fireball — and it exploded, spraying the sky with sparks. We braced for the sound. No sound. The mystery of a silent bomb.

A comet in 1946 and the famous Leonid of 1966 were the most spectacular meteor shows in my experience, but both those I saw from lowlands. The Perseid Shower of 1964 we watched in heather, in wilderness, very near the fire. Wild earth and wild sky. We watched on into sleep.

Tuesday morning, scrambled eggs (powdered) and cocoa-coffee. Sky blotched with cirrus, the pale sun not warm. No matter. Where we were was where we wanted to be. Above our middle world of flowers and parkland, the high world of Glacier Peak ice; below, the low world of White Chuck forests — and why can't the Forest Service understand the three worlds are one?

The trail climbed through alpine firs onto Glacier Ridge and swung across a field of avalanche lilies into the next valley — none other than Pumice Creek again. Green lawns swept from tumbling water to sky-etched ridge. Girls whooped and yelled, Tasha wagged her flag and panted, eager.

Not all was green. Most was white. Our ultimate objective had been Fire Creek Pass but in this wintry summer Pumice Creek — on high as down low — would have to be our home, and why not?

The door was less than wide-open. The trail vanished in steep snow, a cliff below. Betty and I had been carrying ice axes since the Climbing Course of 1948; this trip, for the first time, Penny was allowed one too. That left Becky, who was no problem, and Claudia, who was. We roped for the steep crossings — and Claudia slipped twice, both times held by the rope. We figured we wouldn't be bothered with heavy traffic. For all the rest of the week Pumice Creek was ours alone.

White paintbrush.

Except for the natives. Tasha gave a deep-throated "woof!" and raced over snow, boulders, creeks, scree, a half-mile away in a blink, a furious brown dot charging into a whistling meadow. The high country had cured her wheezes and shivers.

Now, dogs don't belong in Wilderness Areas any more than in National Parks. But so long as horses, hunters, and miners are allowed in Wilderness Areas I see no reason to deny Tasha. She's never caught a marmot or even gotten close enough to have her nose nipped. On balance, she's their friend: keeps them in training for dodging coyotes and the heavily-armed subhumans who shoot anything that can't shoot back.

Water, meadow, snow, old metamorphic rocks mixed with new volcanic rocks — the high origins of the Pumice Creek whose lower reaches we knew well. A good world, a good home. Only where was our house? The sky said it better be stormproof.

After lunch we wandered steep heather and grass and flowers beside the tumbling creek, searching for Camp 3. Everywhere level was snow. Upward more to Pumice Creek cirque, trough of an ancient glacier. All snow.

At the lip of the cirque a buttress jutted out like the flying bridge of a ship. From the brink I looked down, down to forests and out to Pugh and White Chuck and other peaks. And also down 30 feet to a waterfall frothing from under snow

Avalanche lilies.

over rocks perfectly placed, between plantings exquisitely chosen, a masterpiece of landscape gardening. (Ever since Betty has been trying to build a copy on Cougar Mountain.)

The summer before we'd spent a week at Many Waterfalls Camp under the north face of Goode. We called the buttress One Waterfall Camp. Stormproof? No chance. But spectacular, inevitable. And there was no other choice.

The dinglestick fireplace was on bare rock of the buttress. The water supply was the top of the waterfall, reached by careful steps over snow, down a rock staircase, into delicate water-loving plants. The wood supply was bleached bones of alpine trees and shrubs torn from cliffs by avalanches. The tarp and bed were on bumpy, not-too-steep heather between buttress and snow.

A red sunset burned away cirrus. More hung on the Olympic horizon west. But when things are going great nothing can go wrong. I stashed the family under the tarp for safekeeping but slept outside myself, looking for another night of the Perseid, fearing no evil.

Some 40 meteors in an hour, several with aftertrails, and that was the good.

Claudia disturbed my Perseid, crying-complaining she was wet. Absurd. Clouds were dimming the upper fires but my sky-watch bed was dry, no rain so far. Others awoke grumbling. I yelled concise instructions about making do and shutting up

and not bothering people who had meteors to study. They did, more or less. I drowsed off.

A splat on forehead. Ignore it. Another splat. Six more. Can't ignore them. Wake up enough to put on glasses and inspect the sky. No sky left. So under the tarp to join a squirming, whining, cussing gang of girls. Maladjusted. Only now I began to get wet. And not from misting and dripping sky.

By flashlight I examined our house. The ground had been bone-dry in afternoon, yet now water was flowing. From where? By flashlight I studied our neighborhood. All day the cirrus-thinned sun had been subtly warming the up-slope snowfield. Now in night the delayed-reaction meltwater was trickling.

With ice ax I tried to engineer a drainage canal; rocks and topography defeated me. I dug sumps and instructed Betty to bail them periodically; the bailing interval got down to 2 minutes and she said the hell with it.

Steady rain had begun. No escape from our meltwater bed. What a Puritan Father and Eagle Scout can do I had done. Yelled I, "Shut up and go to sleep!" Each Manning contorted around the streams, trying to stay on dry hummocks — boulders thinly fleshed with heather.

Tasha began whimpering and wandering. Rumbles startled me awake before I realized they were jets — and *damn* the noise pollution of wilderness by airplanes louder than thunder or volcanoes. Who slept?

Wednesday dawn of high sun and low fog. Beautiful to dream on. Back to sleep, expecting a glory of a morning. But there wasn't any morning, only cold blowing gray. Penny and Becky crawled out of the trickles and boulders and built a fire and huddled over wind-fanned flames, shivering. Fog in valley, fog in sky, fog all around. And snow. And one loud waterfall. All the world else destroyed. Cook a pot of Wheatena, drink cocoa-coffee. Groggy and listless Girl Guides dried sleeping bags and scorched socks. What was the weather doing beyond the fog? One Waterfall Camp was wide-open to southwest blasts. We re-rigged the tarp closer to the buttress and farther from the snow — rocky and steep ground but no trickles. But even less protection against storm.

Our home was in naked land above trees. We could only survive with fire, much fire. All the bleached sticks near camp were burned. Off into the cirque to scavenge more. Along a narrow strip of soaked meadow between snow above and snow below, then up a steep green slope to the foot of dim-seen cliffs.

Good scavenging; I brought home armloads of twigs and sticks and logs. And then woke the napping females and encouraged them to go for more, telling of the 25 different flowers in bloom, the color that lived still in close-to-ground horizons. They went, and I crept under the tarp and piled up their sleeping bags into a soft mattress and slept a luxurious afternoon sleep. Occasionally the sun broke through briefly, and shreds of blueness—tainted with cirrus. Perhaps we'd used up our luck.

That night Tasha was restless. Something going on somewhere. An alarming flare in the fog. No thunder, though — too far away. After Many Waterfalls Camp the summer before, we were nervous about electricity.

Thursday, a fog-drizzle. Who could remember sun? Warmth? Our buttress, our one waterfall, our family were all that remained of universe and humanity. Lunch for breakfast, under the tarp. At noon the drizzle diminished, we crawled out and built a fire and had breakfast for lunch, hotcakes and strawberry jam.

There are fogs and fogs. Yesterday's fog had been dark and close, a world-destroyer. Today's fog offered hope the sun might still exist. Time to stretch legs. But not Betty's — camp lassitude had prostrated her. Away we went, camp obliterated within a dozen steps. Along soggy meadow into snow, past blocks of schist streaked with jagged white bands of feldspar— pretty rocks, something for the eye to focus on. Then nothing but white snow, white fog. Girl Guides wondered where we were, how far we had to go, can't we go back to Momma now? A little farther, just a couple more steps.

Flat floor angled into a slope. Plug steps in steep snow. A rounded rock rib loomed. Climb onto the crest, pausing to build Stonehenge-like "mysteries" with slabs of gray-weathered andesite.

A vision above. Quickly, now, upward from white and gray into bright-blooming heather fields — red heather first, next white heather, and highest of all, yellow heather. And white-and-blue phlox and purple elephant's head and more, and more. The slope rolled into a broad saddle. On the other side was the edge of the Ptarmigan Glacier; for the first time in their lives the girls walked on a glacier — but not far because crevasses began a few yards away. In soft dirt between flowers were fresh tracks of goats; the girls found wool in juniper clumps and got up a game to see who could gather the most. Pedestals of moss campion were the greenest of green against brown dirt, tiny dot-blossoms shocking violet against the green, the brown. A fog hole opened over the glacier, and another up to clear hard blue with no upper clouds, the first pure sky since the Perseid at Glacier Creek. Yells and hollers into the cirque, down toward sackout Momma, telling her the good news. Tomorrow was our last-chance day, our final day in Pumice Cirque, and the prospects were grand.

No long campfire that night, early to bed in a sudden chill that fire could not dispel — nor sleeping bag. Shivers under the tarp. By morning the meltwater trickles from our neighborhood snowfield were crystals of sparkling ice.

At dawn I poked my head from the tarp to check the weather. Fog had settled onto the river, a long white snake. But later, check again, and fog was only hundreds of feet below the buttress and rising, swallowing trees. Out west the summits of Pugh and White Chuck were warm islands in the sun-gleaming cloud-sea.

By getting-up time fog billows were rolling over camp — separate billows, not a solid deluge. Now we were in warm sun, now bright mist, now sun again. This was the day for which low-valley rain and Kennedy Ridge thirst and high-cirque fog were the preparation. This was the summit day.

To the saddle again, all of us. Then upward more, climbing knee-deep grass and flowers, rich perfume of blue lupine, to the 6952-foot summit of Pumice Peak. Fog billows climbed

too, wrapping us in blind blowing white, opening again to the two-mile-high radiance of Glacier Peak, the last wild volcano. And back down our home valley of Pumice Creek to White Chuck forests and beyond to friendly front-range peaks remembered from climbs past, Pugh and Whitechuck, Whitehorse and Three Fingers, Black and Sloan and Bedal and Big Four. And across the deep broad gulf of the Suiattle River to gardens of Miner's Ridge and beyond to wild giants, summits of adventures past and dreams continuing, Dome and Spire and Buckindy and Bonanza and Eldorado and more mountains than could be climbed or even dreamt of in a lifetime.

Cirrus again was thickening the sky, cooling the sun, but cirrus be damned; we had our summit view to go with forest views and flower views and fog views. All three worlds of Glacier Peak wilderness we had known, and the trip was full and complete.

We stayed long into afternoon, nearly to evening, and lingered down, stopping for the lupine perfume, the yellow heather-white heather-red heather, the goat wool, the andesite slabs, the gaudy blocks of schist. Only once we went fast, on the snows to the cirque floor, where Betty accidently taught the Girl Guides the sitting glissade. Clumsy Momma was fretting over the steepness, wondering how to get down. She slipped and fell and the girls thought it was on purpose and followed her track, sliding half-a-thousand vertical feet

Sloan Peak from Lost Creek Ridge trail.

in seconds, scraping up clouds of snow dust, squealing and howling.

In evening, clouds and fogs melted away, all was calm and friendly. The moment for the special holiday treat developed by mountaineering engineers over 16 years of painstaking experiment. I built the holiday machine: a hole in the snowfield, a sheet of plastic, a layer of snow and salt, and a pot of pudding mix. Strawberry sundaes for desert. Happy sleep that night, serene.

Mountain morning number seven. Wheatena and cocoa-coffee. Dismantle the tarp, pack up, clean up. Then fuss around, delaying. One Waterfall Camp was our home. Here we would live in peace and roam no more.

At last, personal farewells to heather bed, to dinglestick and ashes, to left-over wood stacked for another fire someday, to buttress, to our one waterfall. Hoist packs and away, down into the valley.

Air view of Glacier Peak from the east, the Chocolate Glacier in center.

Image Lake and Glacier Peak.

CHAPTER 2

Prince Creek

At 2 a.m. the world began coming to an end. Tasha had been pacing the floor more than an hour, whimpering. Now Claudia (almost 7) and Li'l Harvey (2½) rushed from their room next door. Moments later, amid a rapid-fire succession of slammed doors downstairs and up, Penny (13) and Becky (12) arrived. Tasha, shaking and panting, committed the unthinkable — she leapt onto the bed. Except for cats and chickens, the entire population was huddled in the safest place there was — Momma's Bed.

Out the window, shocking views of lit-up Lake Sammamish. (Count "one-thousand-one, one-thousand-two," until the sandstone foundations of Cougar Mountain rumble.) About 2:30 I forced an aspirin into Tasha's throat and she gulped and drooled and kept on shuddering.

I wasn't surprised. I'd long been aware of a Malice in the universe and this was a special occasion, my birthday; a few months earlier lightning struck the tallest Douglas fir on our 3-acre estate — obviously a ranging-in shot for my birthday party.

A loud flashing hour of near misses. The storm moved off. The troops drifted to their beds. Tasha curled on a rug, an aspirin-drugged wreck. Altogether an unsettling prelude to the great big all-family week-long high-country expedition scheduled to begin later that day — especially considering what happened to us 3 years earlier at Many Waterfalls Camp.

The Lady of the Lake *at Stehekin, near the head of Lake Chelan.*

The logistics of expeditions are complicated when one of the party is too small to carry a load and too big a load to carry. The previous summer we hauled the Boy 9½ miles from the Chiwawa River road-end to a basecamp for roaming at Buck Creek Pass, in the Glacier Peak Wilderness Area. Betty and Penny took turns with the kiddy-pack and in mid-week I ran the 19-mile round-trip to the microbus for extra supplies.

Now he'd grown into heavy baggage, but also was able to stumble several miles a day — if the miles weren't too tough. That's partly why we picked the Chelan Crest: the road tops out at 6,500 feet, one of the highest points cars can go in the Cascades; wheels would do the hard work of lifting him to meadows.

There was another reason. Several years before, during a year without a summer, some of us civilized ex-climbers had despaired of pleasant hillwalking on the Cascade Crest and driven east. Not with expectations of interesting alpine country. We'd long looked up from the *Lady of the Lake* to the ridges and judged them hot, rocky, and unappealing; the maximum hope was *dry* alpine country. Well, the Cascade Crest was saturated that week but only "empties" clouded the Chelan Crest sky. And we found more than sun — some of the grandest meadow-romping in the range, and a highland that melts free of snow a month earlier than the Cascade Crest. Altogether splendid terrain for fumble-legged 2½-year-old boys.

So that's why, on 16 July 1966, celebrations of Bastille Day and St. Swithin's Day completed, the Manning Gang headed east, shaken but not completely shook by my birthday storm. Two parents, four children, one dog.

We have a family fondness for Lake Chelan. The hamburgers are the heartiest, the milkshakes the creamiest, the horizons the richest. A holiday lunch at a drive-in, then the microbus shifted down and climbed through irrigated orchards into sagebrush and lichen-gray scabrock, into brown grass scattered with tough pines, the cool-blue sun-sparkling lake falling away. Now subalpine forests and now parkland—5,500 feet the microbus gained from Lake Chelan to Navarre Camp. That evening we looked out to twinkle-lights of lowland farms. In our bags we burrowed deep to escape winds sweeping the open ridge, spattering the tarp with rain. What happened to the sunshine-country theory?

Morning was clear, though. Sort out food and gear for the coming week. Hoist packs (all but the Boy). Walk along the west slope of 8,200-foot South Navarre Peak, a shaggy boulder heap haunted with skeletons of a silver forest. One mile contouring rock gardens. A break-your-heart mile of tight switchbacks losing the elevation, the flowers, the views, falling into forests of Safety Harbor Creek. Two steady-grinding miles regaining the losses, emerging into meadows of Miners Basin. I dropped pack near the old cabin, collapsed since my last visit. Check the sky, full of soft vapor clouds, harmless.

Then downtrail to find the gang. Sacked out, unsmiling, by a creek at the lowest point in elevation and spirits. The Boy had walked the flat mile and the down mile but now was rebelling; it was his vacation too and he wanted to spend more of it dabbling sticks in mud. Morale of the Girl Guides, carrying heavy packs at a stick-dabbling pace, was wrecked. So, with Boy perched on my shoulders, again I climbed. Now and then he'd lean over and whisper confidentially in my ear, "Let me down." A bit of walking, then up to the shoulders, then the confidential whisper again. At 4 o'clock, 5½ hours from the microbus, all were assembled in Camp 2, rigging tarp, gathering wood, dabbling, fooling around.

After supper Tasha and I wandered west to a ridge overlooking the Chelan Trench; down the slot of Lone Fir Creek, a glimpse of the lake, hidden the rest of the week by front spurs.

Twilight on the side of Ferry Peak. Barely heard in the high quiet, a trickle of water — uncommon on these dry west slopes. Just here a promontory. And on a tiny flat where a camp should be if anywhere for miles around, an elaborate fireplace, the backwall a four-man stone and the other rocks, carefully fitted together, almost as large; someone had spent much time and muscle.

When? Branches of a whitebark pine more than a foot in diameter crowded the rockery. I dug into the firepit, through needles to humus, and uncovered no trace of ashes.

Already night, now, on Lake Chelan, 6,000 feet below. Tasha whimpering. How old was the pine — 40, 50 years? Things grow slow on sunset slopes. More like 60, even 70 or 80. So near the fire, it couldn't have seeded until the camp fell into disuse. Who huddled by flames here so long ago? A shepherd and his Tasha-like dogs?

Monday morning again was clear. But as we packed for the 3-mile haul to the next camp, white wisps floated overhead,

Betty makes mountain music on the recorder.

then a solid front of gray stratus with brown buttocks — oominous.

I don't know if the Chelan Crest gets more lightning than the main Cascades, but the ridge-top scenery is notable for silver-and-charcoal snags. I wasn't about to set out on the high, exposed trail in conditions that might require a run-like-hell escape — not with a stubby-legged Boy.

Up the trail, alone, for a sky-view west. The doom-shaped front was passing over, doing no evil. In its wake, still beyond the Cascade Crest, was a thick mass. Between the two, an interval of blue. I sat for a while, judging the speed of the system, and guessed we'd have several hours of blue, enough to reach Camp 3.

At various paces we climbed from sheltering trees into the open, flowery basin and over the ridge — marked at the crest by a dramatic snag of a whitebark pine, four sub-trunks and a dozen main branches and a thousand twigs, all silvered and stark and chilling. Drop pack and return for the Boy.

The snag is the entry to the roving country. The trail angled downhill above snug meadows at the meandering head of Safety Harbor Creek; beyond rose the two peaks of Navarre; sun glinted on the distant microbus.

A hillside lawn shaded by greening-out larch. For me, all my early hiking and climbing in the Olympics and on west slopes of the Cascades, every encounter with the two special trees of the rainshadow is a discovery — the full-bodied whitebark pine, the lace-branched larch, the evergreen that is not, losing yellowed needles in fall, sprouting fresh-green needles in spring.

Below the bench, a snow patch and a creek. Time for cheese and pumpernickel and peanut butter and nuts and dried apples and candybars. Then down a little, up a little, to a saddle opening west across the Chelan Trench (the lake not seen, but felt) to 9,511-foot Bonanza; close by the peak, in the valley of Railroad Creek, tailings from the abandoned Holden Mine, poisonous wastes that even at this distance were a garish brown slash in the green-blue valley. The cloud-layer west was thickening and lowering and nearing; our blue-sky interlude was about over.

Switchbacks up the pebble-and-flower shoulder of a small peak, a traverse into the pass between Safety Harbor Creek and the East Fork of Prince Creek. Whoops and shrieks. Below was our new home, the lush-green park, the rounded peaks, an infinity of wandering. And a meadow pond: cried the girls, "Swimming!"

Blue-sky time was gone. Monster billows drifting in. So the rainshadow makes up for the lack of fog with an extra measure of fire and fear? After convoying the group down a snowfield I set off at a run to locate Camp 3. A superb creek rushed through grass, and downstream were alpine firs for wood and shelter. A cold shadow clutched me; a cumulonimbus towered over the ridge. I wove in and out the trees. Bumpy ground, marshy ground, nothing flat and dry. The shadow deepened: at the heart of the fire-rimmed cloud was dense blackness. There'd be more snags when this afternoon's work was done. The Malice of my birthday storm was relentless.

In a bend of the creek, at last, a bit of dry flat ground with shrubs for tarp anchors. The troops arrived. The cloud filled the sky. As I was pegging tarp corners, the first drop hit my fore-head — and splashed my whole face wet. A splat in the grass, a splat on the tarp, a splat on bare dirt, stirring an explosion of dust. Soon the noise would begin.

Tasha, who senses thunderstorms three counties away, seemed oddly concerned. She was right. A dozen splats and the thunderhead lost its heart of darkness and turned clean-white through and through, drifting east, melting. Following billows were mean-looking over the Cascade Crest and probably raising hell there, but the Chelan Crest was the end of the line, only wisps surviving east to the Methow.

The kids had not been properly impressed. Even amid the splats they were stampeding toward the lakelet.

I don't remember at what age dabbling in mudpuddles and splashing in ponds ceases to be the prime goal of any vacation, but I was beyond it and so was Tasha. We went touring hillocks and vales, lawns and shrubs, springs and boulders, loitering 1½ miles to the pass leading to the Middle Fork of Prince Creek—more of the same.

Back at the pond, the girls had begun by wading the grass-clumped shore, squeezing mud in their toes. Penny and Becky grew more daring, exploring water nearly to their hips. Claudia was happiest close to land but I wanted a picture of all three in the middle; with a big sister on each side, kicking and screaming she was dragged to deep water, over her waist. The Boy was not a wader, but several feet from shore was a grassy island just his size. He saw more than an island. He wanted it. Sisters carried him out. All afternoon he sat there, content, "sailing his boat."

Sun stayed late in our west-facing valley, but finally slipped behind Old Maid Mountain. The pond cooled. We gathered at camp. So did mosquitoes. I hadn't noticed them while rigging the tarp. Nor had the kids while churning the clear pond to brown murk. Now we noticed. Just here the loud creek flowed into quiet meanders across a marsh. Some water oozed into the pond and some into potholes and oxbows. The grass was knee-high, the black earth squishy, and the air loud with wings. Was paradise lost?

Beyond the pond rose a dry knoll topped with a cluster of firs. I walked up and sat in the sparse greenery, taking a bug census. Not many, and very tolerable, especially with the evening breeze. Pull down the tarp and drag it up the knoll and re-rig Camp 3.

A broad flat undulated a quarter-mile west before dropping abruptly into forests, beginning the 5,500-foot plunge to un-seen Lake Chelan. In the sunset the flat glowed with paint-brush in prime bloom. Wandering in odd red light from ground and sky, I found two sheep camps. One was perhaps 50 years old: a square of rotten logs marked the site of a tent frame; large trees grew within the square. The other was new and demanded hours of digging a pit with ice ax and stomping cans with boots, burying the junk and cursing the Forest Service for continuing to allow sheep to graze here. "Hoofed locusts," as John Muir called them, have chewed and trampled large areas of delicate Prince Creek meadows nearly to dust-bowl desert.

Camp 3 was Permanent Basecamp. Until the end of the week, a lifetime away, no heavy packs on backs. Tuesday

Young mountaineer with mother and dog.

morning the girls had more splashing to do and the Boy more sailing. Tasha and I went for a walk, ascending meadows to-ward the high peak dominating the basin. Partway up, a felsenmeer, a "rock ocean" of frost-riven blocks black with lichen. From below I'd noted a strange geologic phenomenon — whitish zigzags across the black felsenmeer, for all the world like switchbacks. As if anyone would ever have reason to build a trail here! But they were switchbacks, constructed with toil and trouble long, long ago. The trail climbed nearly to the summit before descending east. On top was a cairn with a register saying "Switchback Peak, 8,200 feet." The register had been placed in 1946; Tasha and I were the third party to sign in.

Opened eyes now spotted remnants of trails crossing every pass, traversing nearly every ridge. How long ago were they built? When was Switchback Peak part of a main route from Prince Creek (and Lake Chelan) to Foggy Dew Creek (and the Methow River)? Was it 50, 70, 90 years ago? As Cascades high country goes, this is old. But nowadays virtually unknown except to the locals, the trails little-used and mostly abandoned. Yet I looked out over more good-roaming meadows than there are, for example, in all of Mount Rainier National Park. With a summer roaming season a full month longer. And the weather far better.

North were miles and miles of rolling parklands at 6,500-7,500 feet, and peaks high but gentle, sloping plateaus scal-loped on east and north by ice-abandoned cirques which now shelter small snowfields. West beyond the Chelan Trench lay the Cascade Crest — socked-in solid. Here, evaporating clouds were merely picturesque. East, cold streams fell from snow-fields into the brown Methow valley.

To the west, soaking-wet hikers were lamenting the rain. To the east, parched ranchers were plotting irrigation projects. Me and Tasha, we kept cool eating snow.

Sprawled on mile-and-a-half-high summit rocks of nonde-script igneous or metamorphic material. An odd pebble at my feet. Pick it up — pumice! The summit was littered with ash blown from Glacier Peak 12,000 years ago. Clouds now obscured the volcano, 30 miles west. A fine grandstand this would have been for the show. (Opened eyes later saw pumice all through the meadows; in creek bottoms were alluvial beds many feet deep.)

Wednesday the pond still fascinated the gang. Tasha and I rambled north to see what we could see. In parkland, now and then a bit of alpine forest, over the divide and down to the Middle Fork Prince Creek and upward to the saddle above the North Fork. The call of the horizons was strong, I wanted to keep going all the way to Stehekin, completing what one day will be recognized as an American classic—the Chelan Crest Trail. But the next stretch was a 1,500-foot drop and camp was already 5 miles behind and the weather had turned scorching. And clear — for the first time Glacier Peak appeared west, Rainier south, and Cascade Crest peaks bright and sharp.

On the return, a side-trip to Boiling Lake, expecting from the name a Cascades version of Death Valley. But no. Through fringing trees into a green basin and waters wind-rippled and sparkling. Tasha went wading, cooling her belly. From bottom silt small bubbles rose through crystal water — the "boiling", I guess.

A quick climb to Horsehead Pass. Several miles down to the east forest ends and brown ridges begin. In another several miles is the Methow River. Beyond rises a baked highland, and beyond that a quantity of air at the bottom of which runs the Columbia River, and beyond that, lost in haze, the Columbia Plateau. The coolness of Boiling Lake is very near all that heat, the greenery of the basin near all that brown; the Chelan Crest is dry compared to the Cascade Crest, but a miracle of lushness contrasted to Methow hills a short hike away. On the east slopes is a boundary zone, an intriguing mixture of alpine plants and "desert" plants. Rising high between Lake Chelan and the Methow River, the Chelan Crest has its feet in two worlds.

For all its loveliness, Boiling Lake is a threat. Fish swim there

Motor Mouth and Tasha.

and in nearby streams and thus the trail from Navarre Camp is becoming scored by wheels, littered with garbage, the meadows rutted, the springs scummed with oil. One of the wheel-crazy idiots was in the Middle Fork valley. We never saw him, but we heard him. A thousand walkers could have been down there and I'd not have been aware of their presence; this lone loud fool, razzing back and forth, used up the quiet of the entire valley. (In answer to my impassioned letters on the subject, the serene Forest Service "doesn't see any conflict" and intends to continue allowing motorized vehicles on the Chelan Crest Trail, and indeed has newly improved access trails for easier motorcycling.)

Tuesday and Wednesday had been glory-romps for me and Tasha. The rest of the gang? They'd exhausted the pond but were suffering from so serious a case of camp lassitude they could scarcely move. Thursday morning, therefore, I commanded: "You will now proceed directly to Boiling Lake. You will enjoy yourselves. That is an order." They wheedled, "What about Li'l Harvey?"

Trickery was required. The lake was too far for him and he was not happy when separated from Momma and the Girl Guides. So the family left camp in a bunch, then gradually strung out. Perfectly normal procedure. He didn't catch on that the female Mannings had pulled a sneak and left us alone.

At the South Fork-Middle Fork pass, two Harveys proceeded west and up to Old Maid Mountain. On this hottest day yet the climbing was slow through hummocks of grass and tiny flowers, but except for brief piggybacks he walked all the way. When his 2½-year-old devotion to alpine conquest dwindled, I'd find the deep shade of a whitebark pine along the ridge crest, or the thinner shade of a wispy larch, and we'd rest. On the north exposure were remnants of snow cornices; at each stop I'd fetch a pile of "no" for him to squish in his fingers, dripping meltwater into dust, making mud to stir with sticks. During one rest he built an elaborate "house," laying out stones in a geometric pattern and explaining that here was his bedroom, here was his fireplace, here was his toilet.

Several times he remembered. A forlorn look: "Where's Momma?" And the answer, "We'll see her in a little while. Just have to walk a little farther." That was okay until the next remembering: "Where's Penny?" And then "Where's Becky?" And "Where's Claudia?" Always, "We'll see them in a bit — just a few more steps."

With five "no" stops we conquered the 7,700-foot East Peak of Old Maid Mountain. A clump of tight-woven pines hugged the summit. Tiny flowers poked through a litter of stones; barren as these ridges appear from a distance, close-up they are rich in fine-scale flora.

The fine scale interests 2½-year-olds. The Boy built little things and watched a spider creep through pebbles. The big view he left to me. Again the panorama of the sharp and icy Cascade Crest and the rounded and green-brown-warm Chelan Crest.

And again the wheel-happy lout in the valley periodically intruded his rotten personality into *my* silence. Who is he to pollute the quiet for everyone so he may enjoy his miserable sport? When will Americans feel as shocked by wanton noise as they are by body odor and bad breath?

Time to descend. A faraway shriek. The Boy jerked to attention: "Momma?" Stubby legs kicked up dust. Soon we all were gathered at the pass. The Girl Guides were full of bounce. They'd followed orders and marched to Boiling Lake. Instead of returning by trail they'd adventured into the unknown, taking a shortcut up a bouldery draw, skating in snow and drinking cold water; from "Shortcut Pass" they'd run down a secret stream-gurgling basin ("The greatest part of the whole trip!") and that's when we'd heard the shriek of glee — from Penny, tripping and tumbling head-over-heels in soft grass.

A late lunch, then straggling to camp, side-trips to extra-special waterfalls and flower fields and boulder gardens and marmots whistling at their friend, Tasha. The North Pacific High seemed to be settling in solid; the regular evening breeze dwindled to a rare puff. Mosquitoes stayed up until 10 o'clock, hours past their usual bed-time.

There was more to do. Several great walks remained from this camp and moving north would open others. (Someday the Chelan Crest will gain due recognition; only then, to avoid losing it to the National Park Service, will the Forest Service bar cattle, sheep, and motorcycles.)

Another free day left. But Friday morning dense cirrus loomed on the western horizon, looking like business, and I didn't care to be trapped on this side of the high pass with the stumbling Boy. I dispatched the troops back to Camp 2.

Alone on the knoll above the pond, waters now clear, unmolested by barefoot girls. Here we'd slept 4 nights, cooked breakfasts and eaten suppers. Watched the first-quarter moon grow from a sliver to a slice. Watched stars and satellites and clouds and sunsets. This had been our family home for important days of our lives. Someday we'd come back, perhaps. But however many trips more we took as a family, *this* one we'd never take again. The world would be different when we returned. So would we. We'd be happy at other camps. But we'd been happy here. And this was ending forever.

An eagle circled above.

I broke loose from Camp 3 and climbed to the trail, pausing every few yards to look back, turning into a pillar. A final sentimental journey to the East Fork-Middle Fork pass. I'd

The Boy and mother climbing heather.

walked this way seven times already and this made twice more. Every rock and flower now familiar. Home. Seven times more and 90 times more would be better.

Cirrus approached from the west. Cumulus drifted from the north — fluff at first. Then one cloud boiled a thousand feet above Switchback Peak in several minutes. Was my birthday storm returning for the kill, had the Malice allowed me this trip simply for better sport? As I ran by the lightning-blasted whitebark pine at the upper entrance to Miners Basin, the sky was erupting thunderheads. Swiftly, swiftly rig the tarp.

Two splats, that's all. Again the oominous clouds frittered away in evening.

On the way to Cougar Mountain next night (after hamburgers and milkshakes in holiday town, Chelan) we drove into schmuck at Snoqualmie Pass. The day after, the Cascade Crest caught holy hell. I wonder — did it rain at Camp 3? Did the Malice finally zing a few bolts onto the ridges of Prince Creek, create a few more black snags?

On the trail with the Girl Guides and the Boy.

CHAPTER 3

White Rock Lakes

Mild twilight, darkening forest. Close roar and splash of Downey Creek. Blended smells of trees and ferns and skunk cabbage and river breezes. All familiar, all surprising. Soft trail under boots. Dick and me hiking up the valley we'd tottered down, soaked and bruised, exactly a year ago. The beginning of the new trip seemed a continuation of the old, the months between a blurred and meaningless shadow-show; with one foul-up after another in the jangled mechanics of earning a living, for me it had been a lost year, a year without mountains.

Bachelor Creek by flashlight, exhausted by heavy pack and 6½ miles. But feeling already the peace and the freedom.

Monday, a good, early noon start, loitering along, sun rays in the tops of tall firs and hemlocks — a difference from the year before, when we'd entered the valley in drizzle and exited in cloudburst. A rest stop at our old camp, just short of 9 miles, where we'd waited under dripping trees from Monday to Thursday, learning the gray mood of forest and water; now the river was bright froth and green-delicious pools. Another 1½ miles to trail's end and a late lunch amid avalanche jungle of the North Branch of Downey. Looks up to hazy-distant glaciers and walls of Spire Point and to well-remembered Timbercone Col, impossibly high. Too far, the meadows, for my rubbery legs to try today.

Across the Lower Timbercone to the Middle Branch of Downey. A bed of needles and moss, kitchen on a gravel bar. Dick

Dome Peak from White Rock Lakes.

went exploring and I drowsed in balmy air by the dipper-infested stream, sunlight filtering through the canopy, waterfalls lulling, the first true sleep in a raucous year, nightmares barred by 11 miles of wild valley, only good dreams here.

In shadowed morning the haul began. Elevation of Dipper Camp, 3,200 feet; of the flowers, 3000 feet more. The year before we climbed the 3,000 feet under lowering skies and descended battered and saturated by a 3-day blow straight from the Bering Sea. This summer the Cascades had been nearly bone-dry since late June, and though the North Pacific High was bending as August was ending, the weatherman was sure nothing worse could slip through than weak little cloudmaker fronts. We had no objection to a bit of fog mixed with our sunshine.

Gently-sloping forests of the Lower Timbercone, then logs and young shrubs and open skies of the avalanche swathe, then steep forests of the Upper Timbercone, ending in short cliffs marking the foot of a rocky spine. Beneath the cliffs, another homecoming — Timbercone Camp. Here, when the cold squall struck, we'd excavated a shelf in the dirt with ice axes, rigged tarp with frozen fingers, cooked dinner on a wind-harrassed primus stove. And when the wind fell, the rain stopped, in sunset colors we'd walked into wet-glistening grass; only a few hundred feet above all was fresh-white with snow.

From Timbercone Camp there are two ways to go, left of the spine or right. The year before in crisp bright morning we climbed left through frosted heather into new snow and up to Timbercone Col. This year we were taking our old exit route, dodging to the right, under and around the cliffy corner on game traces through trees and brush.

The year before we hadn't known for sure there *was* an around-the-corner route, and in hard-driving rain and mist were haunted by the dread of a trapped bivouac.

Now, in sunshine, absurdly simple, ridiculously quick, around the corner into flowery lawns, beside a tumble of bubbles and through a breach in a moraine to a rippling pond amid soft moss, sharp-fractured boulders, inlet streams cutting shallow channels in flats of ice-milled sand and rock-flour. Goat tracks in sand and moss.

Late afternoon. Still time enough to walk the short mile to the pass between the Middle Branch of Downey Creek and the West Fork of Agnes Creek — a pass we'd been waiting a year to see again. But the boulder geometry was so clean, the rock so white in moss so green, the snow-water streams so full of head-spinning drink, and it had been so long, so long, the empty and frantic low-country year. Only Tuesday, an eternal week remaining for other wonders, and nobody but goats had ever camped before in the hidden little basin of Mossy-Moss Pond.

Evening. Sitting atop the moraine at 6,100 feet. Looking down and out Downey Creek forests well-known from days of rain, days of sun, to red crags and white glaciers of Buckindy, to sensuous swells and dips of Green Mountain. Out farther, streamers of scarlet cirrus, pink cirrus, golden cirrus, brown cirrus, just a hell of a lot of cirrus; fog would certainly come for a day or so.

Across the valley, rough-and-icy Spire Point. The Fourth of July weekend of 1953, 8 years before, our gang of Mountaineer barbarians fought through Sulfur Creek jungles, up steep valley-wall forests, over frozen snowfields, to that wind-

cleaving splinter; in the summit register we read the names of the mysterious Ptarmigans who were here in the long ago of 1938.

Wednesday morning we laughed all the way from Mossy-Moss Pond to Pretty Rocks Pass — a treasure trove of emerald-green actinolite, black-and-white schists, micas black and silver and gold, feldspars, quartz, and all sorts of good things. Our plan was to exploit the 1872 Mining Laws and stake "pretty rock claims"; exactly at the pass was a cache of particularly superb specimens we'd abandoned during the great escape.

This year we sauntered along a cirque-and-moraine shelf from pond to pass in 1½ hours, and could have done it in half the time except for the hysterical giggling, stopping to compare the ridiculously easy *now* with the dreadful *then*. How long had we spent the year before, in gale-driven snow, sleet, and rain, visibility less than a hundred feet, traversing steep, slick grass, losing footing and sliding downhill, stopping only by ice ax self-arrest? The agony darn near killed us, and we

Air view from above Pretty Rocks Pass, looking down to White Rock Lakes and across the West Fork of Agnes Creek to Dome Peak, flanked by the Chickamin and Dana Glaciers.

wished it would. And now we saw, as we couldn't then, that a few feet uphill from our death traverse on steep green was the easy-walking shelf.

In a better year, the summer of luck, enjoying the joke, sack out for long and lazy lunch at 6,600-foot Pretty Rocks Pass. There once more was Dome Peak, flanked by the Dana and Chickamin Glaciers; beyond, Sinister, Blue, and Agnes.

And there once more, White Rock Lakes. Before, we'd arrived in sunshine at the end of a week of rain and explored the basin an afternoon and a day. Then at 8 a.m. the tarp blew away and we began the 11½-hour escape over Pretty Rocks Pass, barred by the storm from attempting the Timbercone Col route we'd used on the way in.

Cirrus thickening overhead. Out west, dark middle clouds. Now low stratus seeping from the south. Perhaps more than fog, perhaps some drizzle. Why worry? Easy enough to fill a day or two examining heather nooks, ice-polished buttresses, cliff-shored lakes, not to forget the pretty rocks. Afterwards, enjoy all the more the spectacle of Dome glaciers emerging from cloud, catching the first radiance of sun.

Time to end lunch and descend to the basin, several hundred feet below. But hello, a nasty surprise. The tiny White Rock Glacier, the only passage between cliffs above, lake below, had lost its neve in the warm summer; for several hundred feet, naught but hard ice—and danger of death by abrasion and drowning. For a two-man party with heavy packs, without crampons, the crossing was too treacherous. Ditto for lake ice at the glacier toe, perhaps thick enough but streaked with sinister leads of blue water.

Therefore we traversed from the pass, hoping to puzzle a route down by a combination of buttresses and gullies. Good progress at first, then a deep cleft extending from lake water to somewhere high above us. So we climbed, and climbed, and got over the top of the cleft, and by then were on the snow-covered ridge between Downey Creek and the South Cascade Glacier.

There was Mabel Mountain, our 7,340-foot summit of the year before, guardian of the lakes, and only a stroll away, the cleft had driven us so high. Farther down the ridge was Timbercone Peak—worth hiking up someday, we agreed. (We were to recall that offhand thought.) And there again was the broad, long South Cascade Glacier—an oddity among Cascade glaciers of such large size, extraordinarily flat, a genuine "valley" glacier, and nourished by a cirque ringed by relatively small peaks. We remembered arriving at Timbercone Col the first morning of sunshine, stepping into ankle-deep fresh snow tracked by goats, seeing the new-white glacier brilliant below, the warm close cliffs of Le Conte and Sentinel, and beyond, Formidable and Spider, and farther north, Sahale and Boston.

Spider. The summer before three of us had come south from Cascade Pass, dropped two wives (temporarily) at Kool-Ade Lake, continued to a camp on a heather slope below the Spider-Formidable Col, and next day scrambled to the crumbling summit. Sahale. Ten years before, on my first visit to Cascade Pass, I'd climbed that high and easy nubbin. Connections with the horizon gave sustenance in this mountain-starved year.

A simple descent to the glacier floor and a flat and quick walk to 6,800-foot White Rock Col, gasping again at first view 600 feet down to milky-green tarns in ice-sculptured rock, and down thousands of feet more into the enormous hole of the West Fork of Agnes Creek, and across to Dome.

Later in the summer of our Spire Point ascent, two of my companions plus three other friends spent 2 weeks scrambling and climbing south from Cascade Pass to Sulfur Creek. From summit registers they traced the story of what had been a mystery and now became a legend—the 1938 expedition from Sulfur Creek to Cascade Pass by four young members of the short-lived Ptarmigan Climbing Club. The 1953 party, second to travel this section of the Cascade Crest, called it the "Ptarmigan Traverse," and the name stuck.

They also named White Rock Lakes; a flat rock in the outlet stream seemed to them specifically designed for a kneeling naiad peering into sparkling water.

I'm not sure a mountaineer would have time for a naiad at White Rocks, no matter how long he'd been in the hills. There's too much else there. But she'd be no surprise.

The year before, after shut-in valley days of dim and somber green, the sun and new snow and glaciers and peaks and sky and horizons had been blinding, mind-whirling. And then a vision of quiet lakes. Red-glowing air at sunset. The forever incredible magnificence of Dome. Sprawled in heather crunching cucumber slices, sipping Black Label ("Hey, Mabel") beer. An interlude in the otherwhere. Easier to believe in naiads than freeways.

Another year, another rough scramble down scree and black snow and hard dirt, another arrival at 6,194-foot White Rocks. First stop, Naiad Rock, to drink sparkling water.

Clouds were low; the summit of Dome was gone. Maybe more than fog and drizzle coming, but in the benign summer of 1961, with encouraging words from the weatherman, no real danger. Surely nothing like the famous fiasco of 1960, though it was the exact same week; such 3-day blows come, in August, only once in a generation.

Rig the tarp stout—in case—on Old Hemlock Knoll. Not as convenient to Naiad Rock as our previous camp, but safe and secure behind a tight-woven, wind-streamlined thicket. At 4 o'clock, droplets. Could be there'd be much tarp time, sleeping time, tomorrow. Okay—rain sleep in heaven is heaven still.

Cook supper on the primus stove—hard to keep lit in rising wind. Thanks for the thicket. Bad noises on the weather side, several yards from leeward cave. By the time dehydrated potatoes and peas and chicken chunks were chewable the world had been washed away in horizontal rain. Somewhere —about 6 or 7 miles straight up—the setting sun was shining. Not here. Premature night, vicious gusts swirling over and around our hemlock defense, flapping our tarp. And so to bed.

And so to sleep. But not deep sleep, no dreams. Close above thin tarp and hemlock shield was a roar, a horror. In semi-sleep, flinches of fear. The peaks, the glaciers, the valley, the storm—too large, too strong. Old hemlocks had come to terms, belonged. We didn't. Hemlocks could save themselves but not us.

In howling midnight the tarp tore loose.

Said Dick, "Hell! This is where we came in." Crawl painfully into hurricane (hemlocks no help no more) and tie down the

loose corner. Back to watchful semi-sleep.

Through the roar, a "RIP!" Violent flapping, drenching rain in the face. The tarp was finished, all the grommets on one edge torn away, nothing to re-rig with. Fun is fun, but what now of the widows and orphans?

Grab the tarp edge and pull it down, hold it down, fight the wind. Fabric began to stretch. Drips and trickles through the roof. Just in case, remembering, Dick had brought a pair of enormous poly bags: crawl in, grasp tarp, grit teeth to last out the helpless, trapped hours of blackness.

We did. In late morning, hurricane subsiding to gale, even some sleep.

Thursday afternoon. Holding tarp with one hand, with the other eating breakfast and lunch—a chunk of chocolate, a slice of salami. Thinking of the wild, empty, rough, cold country. Studying alternatives. Wind-roar fearsome, rain assaulting and battering. Not a matter of hibernating a little summer storm, we were smack in the middle of another 3-day blow and couldn't last another night here.

With neve on the White Rock Glacier, we'd have repeated our escape of the year before, but there wasn't and we couldn't. No more than last year could we attempt the crossing of Timbercone Col. Downey Creek was closed.

Might drop into the deep hole of the Agnes and survive— assuming we could find a safe scramble in clouds down several thousand steep and cliffy feet.

Much easier to reach forests of the South Fork of the Cascade River. A better idea: the U.S. Geological Survey research hut anchored to naked rock above the toe of the South Cascade Glacier. No matter how tight it was locked, we'd scratch an entry with axes. That was our grim resolve.

Crawl from poly bags, from sleeping bags, from tarp, soaked to the skin even before putting on boots, hoisting packs. Climb mud and muck and snow to White Rock Col, into a fury of wind and rain and hail and sleet. Slog down the South Cascade Glacier, pounds of pack-saturating water heavy on our backs, wind shoving and pummeling, cold rain stealing body warmth, slowing muscles, clogging mind. We weren't going to be killed, but nearly. Two stupid guys. Two years in a row. Two heavens and two hells.

Head-on into rain, staggering blind. An apparition in bleariness. Stop. Blink water from eyes. Two apparitions. Abominable snowmen? Sasquatches? No, the U.S. Geological Survey in person! Wondering if they'd met abominable snowmen or sasquatches.

The first spacemen from Earth to the Moon, exploring a crater and stumbling into the first spacemen from Mars. Neither believing the other was possible. All in clumsy space suits. Incredulous. Trying to communicate with shouts and gestures. That's about how it was.

But strangers become friends in a hurry in a wilderness storm. As a single party we four continued to the hut. No need to unlock the door with axes. Interior space was cramped but by invitation it was home for Dick and me. The dry wooden floor offered a blessed bed.

Strip off gear and clothes and dry out and warm up by the

On the Chickamin Glacier, approaching the summit of Dome Peak.

stove. Mutually explain ourselves. No real explanation for Dick and me. As for the two apparitions, they'd been retrieving an air drop. Now two others flung in from the storm, returning from the gauging station at the glacier outlet; one was Wendell, the leader.

The statistics were appalling. Run-off from the glacier set a record. Instruments at the 6,000-foot hut registered 6 inches of rain since suppertime the night before, and an *average* wind velocity of 40 miles per hour! At White Rock Lakes Dick and I knew we were having it tough; now we knew exactly how tough, by the numbers.

The GS guys began cooking and Dick and I got out our primus stove and packets of dehydrated barf and Wendell told us to put it away and handed us cans of beer. Feeble beer-blurred protests. Genuine non-dehydrated steak and potatoes and honest-to-gosh bread and butter.

It was as if Dick and I had semi-died during the tempest, crossed over to a mid-world, and were being tempted by the Devil to forswear our devotion to the Wilderness Ideal, to accept the Alpine Ideal. We did not give in; from White Rocks to hut had taken us only 1½ hours (longer though it seemed) and another 2 or 3 hours could have brought us to life-saving shelter in valley forests. But neither did we equate Wendell and his crew with the Devil. Hardly. We still opposed huts in wilderness, but we enjoyed the beer, the steaks, the dry sleep, the good company of scientist-mountaineers.

Rain turned to snow. All Thursday night, all day Friday, all Friday night, snow. Nothing to do but stay dry inside, talk about mountains, read, sleep, eat.

Venture to the outside, more Antarctic than Cascade, for essential purposes only.

Saturday noon, snowfall ceased. Total accumulation during the 40-odd hours, more than a foot. Not startling for a winter storm, but a big mess for August.

The 3-day blow was over. The gang de-hibernated and went out in the cold to advance science. But Dick and I were still trapped. Fog was dense and thick. No clues to where, if anywhere, the sun existed. Solid grayness broke apart, shifting, rolling. Partial, momentary glimpses of the base cliffs of nearby peaks white enough for December. And crevasse fields near the hut, berg-flecked lake at the glacier snout, wasteland of moraine, dim-green forests. The line of new snow was close below.

Sunday morning, a somewhere brightness. The bottom of the fog lifted. Views up glacier and down valley. Thank our hosts —our friends—our Antarctic partners. Then off for Timbercone Col and families in the lowlands.

Steep slopes on the traverse from Hut Ridge, then steeper still on the climb. A foot of new snow at the hut, nearly 2 feet above, with drifts to the waist. Safe? Just barely. Now and then whole slopes abruptly shifted an inch or two, pushing against our legs. The angle and temperature a bit more—that would have torn it, being avalanched in summer.

Climb roped into fog, on glacier, total whiteout. Rest on a rubble rib swept bare by wind. We'd rested here the year before —then in wide sunshine, now in close fog.

The heavy hauling was done. From here we recalled a flat traverse of maybe 10 or 15 minutes across the top of a hanging glacier to Timbercone Col. Soon we'd be plunging into the Downey valley.

Traverse in thick calm fog above crevasse to a rock wall. Skirt below, look around the corner. Fog. Cliff rising left, ice-fall dropping right. No memory from last year of cliffs and ice-falls on the route. A hole opened. Was that a col? Yes, a definite col—but too low, a col from nowhere to God knows where. (Remember . . .) I yelled back to Dick, "This can't be the way, we're too far right!"

Backtrack to the cliff and follow it left and up to a notch. Look down a chute into fog. Visibility less than 25 feet. Steep snow, a suspicion of invisible cliffs falling to the faraway echoing roar of a river—which river? Downey Creek? The South Cascade? (Remember. . . . .)

Climb left more, up more, to ice. Dick chopped steps a rope length, then I passed by and kicked upward to a nose-to-nose confrontation with a white-plastered cliff which forced me left. Cat-stepping along the moat between glacier and rock, I looked between my feet and saw a black hole.

Retreat, trembling, all the way to the big crevasse next to the rubble rib, our last for-sure landmark. Discuss sunshine memories of the terrain, results of fog wanders. We'd been too far to the right, obviously.

A second try, farther left. This time I hacked steps up ice to a bergschrund—and gave a shout of delight. "I'm encouraged!" I yelled down to Dick. "Goats have been here today!" Well did we recall arriving at Timbercone Col and seeing tracks running up to the crest of the ridge. Now we were on the hot-shot, certain-sure, high-line goat route.

A closer look. Foul words erupted. Dick, below, wondered. *Our* tracks. Leading to the brink of the black hole.

Black hole be damned. Now I picked a delicate path through the rotten section and around a corner. Dimly above, a ridge-like shape. The col had to be close. We climbed broken rock, scooping snow from handholds, boot-probing for footholds. Then I was able to squirm around a bulge and step into a shallow moat—and sink breathlessly to my waist in drifted powder. On knees, dog-paddling in fluff, to a bouldery gully. Scramble to the ridge. Dick arrived, took a look—at nothing. A narrow crest teetering in gray vastness. Said Dick, "We've got no business up here."

All the way back and down to the rubble rib. Afternoon well along. Discuss, calculate, theorize. Study maps—primitive and useless. Once more, farther yet to the left. Once more, in minutes, intersecting tracks.

Our hosts were surprised to see us again, but not *too* surprised. After another beer, another non-dehydrated supper, an evening seminar trying to figure where in hell we'd been. To head off the rescue party, Wendell radioed a fire lookout, who radioed the Marblemount ranger, who telephoned our wives.

Monday, Labor Day, was brighter. Fog separated into billows, blue sky between. As we reached the rubble rib Dome broke out, and Mabel, and Spire, and Pretty Rocks Pass, and the gleaming South Cascade Glacier.

We admired the intricate system of tracks we'd created the day before. (Later, talking to Wendell, I learned how very much he and his crew enjoyed the visible history of our confusion.) Twice on the first try we'd been close enough to Timbercone Col to hit it with a snowball. On the second try we'd climbed within another snowball throw of the 7,300-foot

The Spider-Formidable Col, at the head of the Middle Cascade Glacier.

Spider Mountain.

top of Timbercone Peak; a few more steps and we'd have seen the summit cairn built by our GS friends.

Over the 7,040-foot col, down snow-slippery talus, down meadowy moraine. Sun was winning at last. Fog dissolving, the last scraps hugging pockets of dampness on ridge slopes. All the peaks free and clear. Heather warm and dry to sit on, looking.

Bask in meadows, eating blueberries. On a nearby ridge, coyotes howling like women in pain. Rejoicing at the sun? Or had they caught a marmot? Alarm whistles everywhere around.

Down and down, filling up on blueberries. Slow, slow. This trip had cost me $200 in lost wages during an episode of family poverty when creditors were closing in for the kill. But without it, my only long high walk of the year, there'd have been no point in *having* a 1961.

Down the timbercone to a sackout lunch at the crossing of the North Branch of Downey, watching a trout dart this way and that in a pool, looking up to Timbercone Col, impossibly distant. Then 10½ miles of Downey Creek forests, storing up trees and ferns and mosses and drinks of cold water for the coming winter.

It's lucky Dick and I aren't paranoid. The splendid summer of 1961 was marred by only one bit of fierce weather from late June into October. Ours. The White Rocks blow of 1961 even topped the White Rocks blow of 1960; together, they were two of the worst August storms in recent Cascade history. For 16 days effort, we had a total of 1½ days walking-around-time at White Rock Lakes.

We immediately began planning a return. Hearing this, representatives of the mountaineering community implored us to reconsider.

Chapter 4

Many Waterfalls Camp

Ice River Falls.

Claudia was weeks short of her third birthday when she joined the gang on her first backpack. "Motor Mouth" insisted on all the rights and privileges of big sisters Penny (9) and Becky (not quite 8), who were carrying their own gear plus a share of the food. A pack she demanded so we hung a rucksack on her shoulders and she trundled proudly along the Stehekin River trail, sack dragging the ground.

Our objective was modest — Basin Creek, several miles from road-end at Cottonwood Camp. Before we got there Claudia abandoned the rucksack; being bitten by unfriendly bushes wrecked her morale. Camp, though, was free of nettles and had lots of water to splash in, throw rocks in, dabble sticks in.

Next morning we climbed toward Cascade Pass, which I knew well from the west and long had wanted to approach from the east. The Great Rockslide was a slow struggle. Penny and Becky and I would hike a few minutes and wait and wait while Betty hand-led Claudia up the staircase. On better tread the pace rose to nearly 1 mile an hour — until the cataract of Doubtful Creek. I carried sack-of-meal Claudia over under my arm, steadied older sisters on leaps from rock to rock, and tried to do the same for aged, incompetent mother, who fell to her knees in foam and completed the crossing in a

semi-crawl. "Do it again, Momma!" cried laughing daughters.

The trail swung through cliffs into the hanging valley of Pelton Lake and entered snow; it was mid-July of a cold year. Claudia tried a few slipping and sliding steps and decided she didn't like snow. I explained the principles of the flat-footed tramp walk, but there aren't any tramps that young. Wails of rage. A half-mile short of Cascade Pass we turned around.

Too late. For all her energetic mouth Claudia was a baby. I carried the collapsed lump in my arms. When arms failed, put her down to walk a bit. Eyes close and knees go limp. Pick her up again. Betty fretted whether we'd be able to force life-sustaining soup past the lips of our tortured infant. Tenderly place the sleeping child in bed. And she instantly awoke and for the next 3 hours tore back and forth between campfire and the Stehekin River and Basin Creek, covering as many miles in a dead-run as she'd grudgingly crept all day.

The entire week we camped in the upper Stehekin moist air was flowing from the ocean. We met climbers who'd been sitting for days in fog and drizzle at Cascade Pass. Where we were all the weather was good; rags of disintegrating clouds only improved the scenery.

One day Penny and I climbed into Lower Horseshoe Basin: creeks running through boulders and gravel, lush mosses and low-growing water-side plants, open heather knolls. She found the skeleton of a bear and collected trophies of jawbones and molars. We marveled together at the white lines inscribed on the horseshoe of 1500-foot walls, the waterfalls frothing from snow-fields of Upper Horseshoe Basin, above which rose jagged summits of Sahale, Ripsaw Ridge, Buckner, and Booker—peaks we had seen from the *Lady of the Lake* while cruising up Lake Chelan.

I recalled looking down those waterfalls from the upper basin 9 years before, Penny a 6-months-old baby left home on Cougar Mountain with her mother.

Four of us had taken the high line north from Cascade Pass, climbing Sahale Arm meadows above iceberg-flecked Doubtful Lake, into moraines and ice-scored slabs below the Sahale Glacier, then down the staircase of a narrow rock spur to the basin floor. Except the "floor" was a sloping shelf mostly occupied by snowfields, moraines, and torrents. At the lip, where torrents began the plunge to the lower basin, we camped on a fringe of non-flat heather. Next day we climbed 9112-foot Buckner and looked over the Boston Glacier, one of the largest in the Cascades, to the north wall of Forbidden, and to many-glaciered Eldorado and its distinctive summit, a knife-edge of snow.

I remembered kicking steps along that knife-edge in a Labor Day fog 4 summers before. Couldn't see how far the snow slopes fell on either side but could hear far-below rivers. Walking a tightrope above eternity. What to do if a partner on the rope team falls from the ridge? Instantly jump off the opposite side. A discouraging idea. Fog began to shred. Peaks appeared, half-wrapped in clinging clouds. "What's *that?*" we'd ask each other, puzzling over inaccurate, half-empty maps. The peaks were monsters and so were the glaciers but most were total strangers to us even by name—those that had names.

Startling to learn there were such peaks, such glaciers in the Cascades. Why hadn't they been famous for decades? As near as we could tell, only eight parties, for a total of maybe 20 people, had preceded us to the summit of 8868-foot Eldorado, easy a climb though it is.

And I remembered scrambling in a panic down the west ridge of Forbidden 2 years earlier, running from a black squall sailing over the broad valley of Thunder Creek, crackling with electricity, drawing a bead on us—though eventually it veered to blast Logan and Buckner instead. Ours was the seventh party on 8815-foot Forbidden and we knew personally all but two of the dozen people who had climbed before us. The North Cascades were pretty much a family secret in those days. On the rare occasions we met other travelers at Cascade Pass, usually they were friends, part of the family.

And north from Eldorado, at the far end of a line of nameless rock-and-ice, was 8347-foot Snowfield Peak, which I'd climbed 3 years before on a 4th of July weekend with a Climbing Course group led by Bill Degenhardt. The last party had signed the summit book 17 years before, and the only other party the year before that, and Bill was on both those climbs. Setting out for this high but easy peak above the Skagit River and Diablo Dam, we'd no notion of a third ascent, not so late in history as 1950.

All these peaks and glaciers we admired from Buckner, and cirques and valleys, wild country low and high ringing the headwaters of Thunder Creek, one of the great streams of the range.

Next day we packed over the Buckner-Booker Col to Park Creek Pass and the following day climbed Logan. Again we saw Thunder Creek running west into the Skagit River and Puget Sound. And now we looked down—and *down*—into head-waters of the North Fork of Bridge Creek, under the east face of 9087-foot Logan and the north wall of 9200-foot Goode, down to green fields and white streams. What a fine place that must be to be.

At the same spot a year or two later the same thought struck Dick Brooks. We agreed this was one of the best holes in the North Cascades and we were becoming collectors of holes, valuing them as once we'd valued summits. A trip to the feet of Logan and Goode would be memorable, we thought. How memorable we couldn't have dreamed.

Thinking back, it's odd I delayed my first visit to Stehekin until 1962, the year of our Basin Creek trip. On a pair of 1950 attempts on Bonanza (the second successful) I'd been infected by Lake Chelan, whose water-road approach gave the ascent a distinctive flavor; in my case, though, no raging lake fever developed overnight. But as years passed I climbed peaks and crossed passes along the Cascade Crest from Plummer Mountain and Suiattle Pass on the south, above the main fork of Agnes Creek; to Spire Point and Mabel Mountain and White Rock Lakes above the West Fork Agnes; Spider Mountain above Flat Creek; Slowdown Peak above the West Fork Flat; Magic Mountain and Cascade Pass and Sahale and Buckner above the head of the main Stehekin River; Park Creek Pass at the head of Park Creek; Logan above the North Fork of Bridge Creek; and Stiletto above Copper Creek. From these peaks and passes and others I looked down into headwaters of many streams flowing into the Stehekin River and Lake Chelan. I came to have a curiosity about the place where all these waters gathered into a single flow and entered the long, narrow, fjord-like lake. I came to want to approach the peaks and passes by the classic line, starting at the lake and following the valleys.

Becky helping rig the tarp.

Penny helping rig the tarp.

So in 1962 we docked at Stehekin, every mountaineer's home town. We liked it so well we returned next summer with Dick and Grace Brooks to collect the big hole of North Fork Bridge Creek.

1963, the Summer of Fire and Flies, the maximum for both in many a year. Our family gang was blasted from a meadow camp at Harts Pass on the 4th of July. Later in the month I named a tributary of Sibley Creek "100-Fly Creek" because that was the number of my confirmed kills (no count kept of probables and cripples) while waiting for Motor Mouth, big sisters, and Momma; camped on the side of Hidden Lake Peak we sweated out the edge of a thunderhead that gave us a mere pit-a-pat but terrorized the Stehekin.

The night we camped by the microbus at 25 Mile Creek, flashes and rumbles and a few plops on the tarp. Cruising up Lake Chelan next day on the *Speedway* (the *Lady of the Lake* was full-up), summits lost in gray billows. Yet bursts of light pierced roiling cloud masses, the sun still existed and the pattern of the summer might change. Room for hope.

The Brooks-Manning roadside camp at the start of the Bridge Creek trail was deviled by flies. Run to the creek and escape torment, sitting by the tumult pouring through a narrow cleft, cold water and cold breezes driving away demon wings.

Next day, no escape. Dry forest trail climbed in humid, sticky, stagnant air far from creeks. Salal leaves disgusting, soiled by glistening fly crap. As many flies in the forest as stars in the sky. Hopeless odds, no point in crusading, no chance of victory. Slap only when bitten, crushing obscene beasts into smears of blood—human blood. Walk walk walk to keep the swarm loose —but resin-heavy air was hard to breath, trail steep, pack heavy. Rest—and the buzz crescendoed in vicious glee. No rest.

Everything was confused by flies. I reached the Bridge Creek crossing ahead of the others and crawled under the bridge, in shade, next to rapids and stream breeze. Somehow Dick and Grace and Penny walked over the bridge without my knowing. Much later, wondering where everyone was, I spotted the remainder of the Girl Guides approaching the bridge. A hasty reunion. Then hotfoot uptrail to retrieve Eldest Daughter and post her in the woods to wait; Dick and Grace proceeded on.

Penny alone in the woods, the rearguard golly knows where. I backtrailed to wait at a miserable hunters' camp by a spring trickling from black ooze—cool water but no breeze. Pace up and down, slapping flies. Spread a tarp on the ground and crawl under to hide—heat and humidity intolerable. Outside to gasp sticky air and pace up and down, slapping—intolerable. Run up the trail. Run down the trail. Try the tarp again. Sanity slipping loose.

Screams in the forest uptrail. Run, yelling to save Eldest Daughter, who was running and crying, alone too long with flies and wilderness. Where was the rearguard, where? No time to think. No chance of rest. I ran downtrail and found Motor Mouth whining and Momma wheezing; only Becky could take a step without stumbling, could focus her eyes.

Is God really good? Difficult to believe in fly time. Some religions say the world was created not by God, but by the Enemy of Mankind.

Evening. The Manning Gang assembled at Grizzly Creek, sitting on boulders by cold, fast water, trying to bathe in stream

Rainbow Falls in the Stehekin River valley.

breezes but mostly slapping flies. At least we could splash water over faces and arms and drown the wicked beggars. Cook dinner on the rocks; a bad scene, but a few feet away in trees was worse. Where was the Brooks Gang? Lost to us that night, somewhere up the valley.

Sunset. Cool night. An end of flies—but also a dark cloud and pits and pats and distant noises. (Not so distant from the Brooks, we later learned; their tarp was illuminated and battered.)

Morning. Bugs awoke and drove us out. First, the ford of Grizzly Creek. I scouted the route, a dozen yards of rapids. Face upstream, test the footing, steady the stance with ice ax, swift water boiling to hips. To the far bank, drop pack. Return for 4-year-old Clodhopper, carrying her pack on my shoulder, her under my arm, now and then asking if she'd like to go swimming. ("NO!") Back again to convoy a pack-carrying daughter, and another, and a wife. After nine crossings I liked it so well I was sorry to have to start hiking.

We tried to keep the family in a bunch to face trouble together but flies ruled. Legs went as fast as they could to carry the body away, away; mind lost control. Stifling, sickly-sweet lushness of alders and willows and grass. Eldest Daughter and I moved ahead, looking for water. Had to have water, couldn't wait for the rearguard without water. But no side-streams. In all the valley the only drinking was in Bridge Creek.

Tantalizing loudness. Madness. Drop packs and slash and

stomp and shove through greenery to river gravel, to cold, clear, fast water. Under heavy sun, heavy air, embrace gravel and duck heads in stream. Underwater we were free of flies, we dreamed of developing gills and moving permanently into the river, emerging now and then to mock the flies and maybe eat a few. But we lacked gills and had to come out to breathe. I threw a cup of water in Penny's face and she shrieked. She threw a cup of water in my face and I shrieked. Sit by the stream sloshing each other, washing away flies, each cold shock letting us forget for an instant.

The rearguard, suffering terribly, arrived. We sloshed them and they screamed and joined the sloshing. Strength returned. Up packs and away.

Again Penny and I were bitten into speed. Qualms of conscience, realizing Becky could have kept up but was staying with Momma out of loyalty. (We're not really less loyal than Becky, we're scouting water for poor Momma and them.) But still no side-streams. Break free from a tangle of alder. Deep grass sweeping to the river—a long way off but loudly wet. Drop packs and run. Head-soaking and water-tossing and waiting. And waiting.

Rearguard couldn't be far behind. Brooks Gang couldn't be far ahead. We'd go join the Brooks, that's what we'd do; the rearguard couldn't miss the broad track beaten through grass, bent willows stuck in trail, pointing to water. They'd regain strength and follow in a bit.

So Penny and I sweated onward and upward to the Brooks camp and glad hellos and an end of agony. Flies weren't bad, we'd climbed above trillions into tolerable hundreds.

"Where are the others?" asked Grace. "Not far," said I, heading for the river. Becky arrived, proving the point—but on questioning her we learned the rearguard had missed the turn-off to the water-stop, blindly trampling the markers, and all were near death. Grace, worried, ran downtrail to give encouragement—and returned in a hurry, reporting Betty had collapsed. Almost more ominous, Motor Mouth had stopped talking. I ran down grasslands with a bucket of water. And learned I was due once more to be a father, in about 6 months. Earth Mother hadn't told me yet because such flagrant overpopulation is a crime against humanity. I refrained from pouring the bucket of water over her head—until she asked me to, which she did, so I did.

(Thus our entire family, including the Boy, was at that camp—in the same way Penny reached Camp Muir at the age of minus 5 months and Becky climbed Kendall Mountain at minus 3 months.)

The evening of August 12, 1963.

Many Waterfalls Camp, 3900 feet. Plenty of ice water in the river. Cool air from a close snowfield. Knee-deep wide-open grassland, hundreds of acres of tall grass. No trees; both family tarps rigged from bipods of poles swept down by avalanches.

Now we could enjoy the big hole. Downvalley, beyond Benzarino and Corteo, a long view to 8122-foot McGregor Peak—a friendly landmark seen many times through the years from Cascade Pass. Very near—we'd walked beneath it on the trail—the ice-hung 6000-foot north wall of Goode, third-highest non-volcanic peak in the Cascades, topped only by Bonanza and Stuart. At the valley head, the east face of Logan. On the ridge connecting the two, and immediately above camp, a belt of glaciers; from them, white plumes pouring down cliffs.

6 p.m. A fire going in a dry stream bed, a pot of soup boiling. Blurry clouds had thickened, unnoticed amid other problems. Now a flash and crackling boom and a splat-splat-splat. Dive for tarps—Penny joining the Brooks, who had more room. Dick donned raingear and carried the soup pot around, filling cups. Lying in tall grass drinking hot soup, tensing to occasional flashes, listening to rumbles and steady rattle of rain. In an hour, all calm.

I crawled out, stoked the fire, and put on a pot of water for the main course. Nearly 8 o'clock. Examining the sky, the shifting clouds, bottoms above the summits of Logan and Goode, I saw black places. Evening sun wasn't breaking through: whatever was out west was thick; not a single piercing ray, not a hint of sunset color. I poked my head under the Brooks tarp and said, "Somehow I don't think we've heard the whole story."

I happened to be looking directly at Logan the instant it all began. Sky black. Cloud-bottoms high. And then a strangely-yellowish tongue curled over the summit ridge. Wherefrom this odd cloud, that weird color?

The oily tongue had barely slid over the rim than I was blinded by a bolt striking the peak. One-thousand-one, one-thousand-two, one-thousand-three—WHAM! Sudden, crushing rain. Run for tarp in an explosion of fireworks.

Our tarp was rigged in a line with the valley, open at both ends, allowing a clear view. Bolts hitting all along the Logan crest, quick jets of white flame connecting rock and cloud. Other blazes from cloud to cloud. Continuous fires, three or seven or nine burning at once, thunder a steady rumble punctuated by crackle-crackle-BOOM! Lie on stomach in the grass, watching the catastrophe on Logan.

Violence had begun with that evil yellow cloud which somehow reminded me of flies. Now it poured down the face of Logan, turning dense gray, expanding crazily everywhere. The mountain vanished, the upper cirque vanished. The vile cloud filled the valley from side to side, washing away peaks, and from top to bottom, swallowing trees and meadows. The front was solid and fast. Bolts and flashes constant, no count possible. But from blinding brightness, ground-shaking loudness, we could feel the approach.

Furious gray-black front dissolved the knoll above camp, lashed tall grass into a tempest of green waves. Foot by foot closer through grass. We braced. Hurricane hit. Tarp ballooned, tore at anchors. Horizontal rain swept under the tarp from end to end, soaking bags and gear. Flash-BAM! Flash-BAM! Thunder simultaneous with lightning.

Clutch grass, head down, eyes closed. Becky screamed, "WE'LL ALL BE KILLED!" She was right. The tarp would go any moment. A bolt would find us. We'd drown or burn. Or be stunned to death.

After each world-burning flare just time to think, during the thunder-pummeling, "That one didn't get us." Survive from second to second, dodging one bolt, drawing breath, dodging another.

Hurricane passed downvalley. Now an ordinary gale. The tarp had held. Downpour pressed it against our bodies.

Still Logan was being blasted, and our camp, and now Goode was attacked. Curled in foetus position I watched the assault on a small tower jutting from the wall. Each time the fire hung so long I expected the tower to melt, droplets of molten rock running like candlewax.

Now something new. In split-second intervals between sky flames, streaks of flame on the Goode wall and thudding crashes loud as thunder—huge boulders shaking loose, smashing against cliffs, striking gigantic sparks, battering the mountain into fragments.

And more. Seen in flashes, waterfalls had swollen monstrously beyond peacetime size, were ugly brown floods. Under the thunder and boulder-crash, earth-pounding roar of water run amok.

Always the bombardment of eyes and ears and guts. After hours of terror, weary stupor. Only in the closest bolts involuntary wordless prayers to whatever deity might be in charge. 11 o'clock. Possible now to count one-thousand-one, one-thousand-two between flash and blast. The tarp rose, released from pressure of the monster hand; rain lessened to a cloudburst.

Except for Becky's outcry when the hurricane hit, no word had been spoken. And none now. Separately we slid into exhausted sleep—joining Clodhopper, who had dropped off after the soup and missed the whole show.

Sleep but not peace. Semi-consciousness aware the storm center was nearing McGregor, us under the trailing edge—and again a flash-BANG, another front pouring over Logan. Light and noise grew, rain pressed tarp back onto bodies. But the first assault had drained us of terror. Fear now mixed with boredom. Not that I ever slept deep enough for dreams; that part of me which might have dreamed kept watch.

The second assault marched east to McGregor, rain slackened. And now a third put the blast on Logan. An angry prayer to the Infinite: "Kill us quick or leave us alone!"

A fourth, and a fifth. Each spent about 2 hours with us; as one was leaving, another arrived.

During Number Four dawn lightened the valley. New confidence now night was gone. A bit of arrogance: our North Cascades gods were getting as tiresome as a Wagner music drama. Sleep on, as deep as one can sleep in a power-making factory releasing more energy than all the hydroelectric dams in America and all the atomic bombs ever exploded.

Number Five came in broad daylight. Look to the brown torrents obliterating above-camp cliffs, feel the ground tremble with tons of pounding water. Back to sleep. Storm wasn't going to quit. But as well-adjusted North Cascades citizens, we could out-sleep any storm. (So here comes Number Six, and does it have any tricks? Roll me over, lay me down, we're at it again.)

10 a.m. Lightly dozing. Listening to crashes on McGregor and waiting for Number Seven to bang Logan. Waiting. Bolt-thunder interval increases to one-thousand-seven, one-thousand-ten, one-thousand-fifteen. Rain fritters to pit-pit. A calmness, a serenity, a somewhere-sun. And rain stops.

Creep from tarps, shell-shocked veterans emerging from trenches on Armistice Day. Counting the soup-time overture, we'd been bombarded 16 straight hours.

Brooks and Mannings greeted each other as if separated by years of danger, rejoiced in peace and sun.

Our last-night kitchen was a loud creek. The pot put on to boil at 8 p.m. was downstream, lodged in rocks. Dry meltwater channels through our grassland were rushing with stormwater.

Build a new fire above the new creek and cook a big long breakfast-lunch, making up for the lost supper. Sun dried grass and bags and gear. Luxuriate in warmth and quiet—quiet except for brown waterfalls, which began to thin.

Afternoon wanderings, keeping a weather eye on Logan. I was high above camp, next to a brown waterfall, when I chanced to look east and saw McGregor engulfed by a black mass moving *from the east*. Treachery! My girl gang, in camp, didn't notice the storm—they were fascinated by Big Daddy leaping down snow and meadows and scree as if chased by a bear. I dove under the tarp just as noise and splash began. Dick and Grace, wandering elsewhere, were caught and drenched. But this was a single and quick 2-hour episode. Supper was quiet and dry.

Storm from the west, storm from the east. What next? Three days of intense-blue sky and bug-dispersing breezes, days of roaming the big hole, every bit as good as it had seemed from above.

The morning we left Many Waterfalls Camp, fly-and-lightning weather returned. Chewed by jaws and soaked by cloudbursts and scared by flash-bang all the way home—and all the rest of the summer into October.

One stark memory stands out—even above the hurricane. A half-hour downtrail from Many Waterfalls Camp, the place Penny and I dropped packs the second time and ran to an orgy of drinking and splashing. On the way in, a wide grassy meadow—just like our camp. On the way out, trail was destroyed for 500 feet, buried 6-8 feet deep in boulders and gravel and splintered trees. The entire meadow and all that lived there had been destroyed by a flash flood in the night of the 16-hour storm.

What if it had been *our* meadow?

The Boy and mother plugging through the snow.

Chapter 5

The Great Shuksan Fiasco

"It's sadistic," I told the 1955 Climbing Committee, "to schedule Shuksan on a 2-day weekend. Why do all that driving and hiking and never have a chance to savor one of the great basecamps in the Cascades? Ladies and gentlemen of the Committee," I concluded, "just once let's have fun. Let's climb it Labor Day."

As an elder statesman, my arguments carried weight. "Okay," said the dubious Committee, "on condition *you lead*." Said I, "Done!"

My first time on Shuksan had been a traditional rat-race from Heather Meadows to the summit and back again, flowers and streams and cliffs and glaciers flying by so fast I glimpsed a thousand things that demanded stares.

The following year, in September, I returned with wife Betty, expecting plenty of leisurely staring in the stumbling company of "the most incompetent climber still climbing," as she was known in Climbing Course circles. But Sunday morning was bitter freezing, we couldn't crawl from bags until the sun was up, and the 8 a.m. start left little room for loitering. One odd event: from the Summit Pyramid we spotted a bear on the Crystal Glacier. How came a bear here? Presumably by wandering the ridge from Baker Lake. But now he was descending the icefall to Sulphide Lake. A slip, a slide—nearly into a

Mt. Shuksan from Table Mountain; on the right, Lower and Upper Curtis Glaciers, the latter known as "Hell's Highway".

crevasse. Saved by a skillful all-claws self-arrest. Black shambling beast disappeared over the bulge. Did he make it? I've always wondered why bears climb mountains.

Two Septembers later we carried ropes, axes, and irons to Lake Anne. Sky clear, sun steady, breezes balmy. Four of our five had been to the summit and now awoke singly at dawn and gazed at the 4500-foot rise of warm brown rock and brilliant white ice and went back to sleep. Hot up there. Weather too good for climbing. Dick Brooks was baked awake by sun, tried to start conversation, got no response, and realized he'd been rooked. "But *I* haven't climbed Shuksan," he complained. "I *wanted* to climb Shuksan. I came *specifically* to climb Shuksan." Lazy smiles and chuckles.

A drift toward the lake. A water fight, which Dick pressed with a vigor suggesting residual hostility. Blueberry slowly up the ridge of little Mt. Anne. Belatedly a revival of the urge to conquer. But all the gear was in camp. By odd chance Ted and I found a broomstick left by some earlier hero. A good tool for gouging steps in late-summer snow; on a ticklish pitch I braced the stick against the slope and Ted used it as a railing to lead over the top into a moat, me following on a broomstick belay.

In one direction, 9127-foot Shuksan, in the other, the white volcano of 10,778-foot Baker; the two facing across the valley of Swift Creek. One peak a complex architecture of ridges and walls and hanging ice, the other a simple design of glaciers radiating from summit icecap. A superb pair. Each a classic. Together, with green forests between, a masterpiece.

The 1951 ascent of Anne was my inspiration for the 1955 Experience Climb. I wanted not only to lead students on a fully-appreciative Shuksan ascent but also to Anne. I talked Dick into coming, promising we'd climb for sure this time.

On no other trip I ever led for the Climbing Course did I leave town feeling so relaxed. Weather calm and clear, no threats on the horizon. The route as familiar as the back of my hand—a series of rock and snow and ice delights, never tough but always interesting.

Even checking the signup didn't bother me. I had to admit the Climbing Committee was right. Maybe after 8 years I was civilized enough (over the hill) to throw away a Labor Day weekend on Shuksan, but the barbarians were seeking objectives that would keep them rat-racing the full 3 days. Rope-leaders were notably lacking; I'd have to use one or two not really qualified. And the luxurious schedule had attracted people who saw it as their only hope of ever making Shuksan.

But why worry? Good companions, all 20, and in civilization there is strength.

A second flaw in the Labor Day concept: at basecamp we found two large parties, one from Oregon, the other from the University of British Columbia. Unheard-of congestion. (For 1955.) Yet there was plenty of camping space by the lake and in the cosy headwaters of Shuksan Creek, and doubtless the other groups would start in the middle of the night and be out of our way at the civilized hour I planned for departure.

We stayed up shockingly late for a Shuksan camp, watching alpenglow fade from rough buttresses and massive walls cut horizontally by the Upper Curtis Glacier—Hell's Highway it's called. The summit seemed unattainable—4500 feet above the lake and appearing much more, every access blocked by formidable cliffs and icefalls. In evening I assembled the party, told how we'd start at 6 a.m., a later but better hour than usual, return to camp by 7 p.m., and on Monday stroll up Anne before hiking to the cars.

At 5:30 in mild morning, sunlight on the Summit Pyramid, I gave a loud yell and sank back to sleep in soft heather. At 5:50 I awoke again, ate a doughnut and a can of fruit cocktail, crawled from bag, pulled on boots, stood up, shouldered rucksack, grasped ax, and at precisely the advertised hour of 6 yelled once more and started walking.

Alone on steep trail in cool shadow. Look back to camp, falling away below. No one following.

So much for the experiment. Too many Practice Trips and Experience Climbs, too many yells, too many warnings with clenched fist and brandished ax; I'd wrecked my throat chasing students into Commonwealth Basin blizzards, Rainier midnight gales. Tired of nagging. Couldn't adults get out of bed by themselves? I'd experiment to see if *this* party could move without threats of violence.

It couldn't. I climbed alone.

Pleasant to climb alone. The teacher playing hooky. An interlude of anarchy.

The trail (built by the CCC in the 1930s?) traverses to an overlook beside the Lower Curtis Glacier, fed by avalanches from the Upper Curtis. Before there I left tread, climbed scree to a snowpatch, kicked steps, crossed the moat onto rock, and scrambled to a perch. Await, now, the creeping insect-shapes below, belatedly pursuing their leader.

A balmy-warm perch, relaxing. At last, time to stare.

Across the air-filled gulf of Swift Creek, the morning-shining volcano, crevasses sharp-traced by sun and shadow; beneath glaciers, glowing forests, soft-green texture of gullies and ridges.

I followed the line of our 1948 Labor Day ascent up the Boulder Glacier to the football-field summit. Multiple-use was only beginning in the valley then and the trail started in river-side forests 10,000 feet below the 10,778-foot peak. In those days we climbed the whole mountain, not merely the upper fraction. (Now the river is drowned by a reservoir, the forests moth-eaten by patch-logging nearly to timberline.)

I remembered returning 6 weeks later, from the north, getting lost in logging slash, finding the trail to Kulshan Cabin by flashlight and hiking in a night so cold the creeks were freezing, ice sheathing boulders, icicles stringing from waterfalls. Next dawn, high on the Coleman Glacier, we saw the shadow of Baker reaching in winter-crystalline air across saltwater to Vancouver Island; climbing, we watched the tip of the cone race over bays and inlets, towns and farms, the edge of darkness so clearly defined that for a while one particular barn was in sun while the owner's house was still in shadow. We wondered if the sleeping farmer knew.

A year later, October again, we climbed the Coleman in a narrow layer of clear air between lowland fog rising under us and cloudcap storm raging above. Stumble blindly onto summit plateau. Cloudcap breaks into billows. Sun-torrents flood through chasms. Engulfed for a mind-whirling moment in fire-bright crystals of gale-driven ice.

(I would return to Baker again and again. We'd hike from Schreibers Meadows to Morovitz Meadows, onto Railroad Grade, a moraine crest just wide enough for goats and boots, and upward through ice-polished slabs and waterfall slots and more moraines to the edge of the gorge where the Easton Glacier drops ice blocks into a dark and narrow valley beneath the Black Buttes, steep-crumbling remnants of a volcano older than Baker. And we'd hike from Austin Pass over and around Table Mountain meadows, screes, and lakes and at Herman's Saddle look straight ahead to Shuksan, straight behind to Baker. And we'd return to Kulshan Cabin and camp on a forested moraine above seracs of the Coleman, and roam to higher ice, and Becky and Claudia would wade in a sandy pond under a spray of icewater, and Tasha would harrass marmots.)

The troops were arriving. Nearly 8 o'clock. A lady bawled me out for not personally extracting her from the bag; that's what Leaders are for. The most experienced climber in the party, Dick (not Brooks), wondered about this newfangled leadership technique—was it my plan to climb a mountain or play a game of fox and hounds?

I felt the bitterness of a betrayed anarchist.

Mr. X toiled over the moat, wearing shorts. Asked I, "Why are you wearing shorts?" Replied he, "Want to get a tan." Asked I, "Do you have pants in your rucksack?" Replied he, "No. Weather's real good." Asked I, "Do you have pants in camp?" Replied he, "Yes." Said I, "We do not travel glaciers in shorts. If you want to climb Shuksan, go get your pants. If you don't catch us before we enter the Chimneys, sit down and *do not move* until we come off the mountain."

Mr. X flung his bare flesh downhill in dangerous leaps. Dick (the Brooks), champion of the underdog, listening incredulous, mildly asked, "You wouldn't really send a guy all that way just for *pants?* Said I, fully reverted to primeval nastiness of the Leader, "You *bet.*"

All the party assembled—except Mr. X, stirring trail dust below. Scramble up a heather staircase to a talus shelf. Now for the Fischer Chimneys, leading 500 feet to the crest of Shuksan Arm, an intricate route discovered decades ago by Happy Fischer, thus solving the confusion of bewildering cliffs and clefts. The Chimneys are charming. Once the correct entry is found a gully leads to a ledge, the ledge to another gully, and so on, easy scrambling all the way.

Upward toward the Chimneys. Several clefts. Which one

(only one works) was the entry? I'd been here three times before and darned if I knew. Call a halt, a long, civilized rest. Probe the walls and memory. Nothing.

People in the cliffs! Climb on. But the people were descending. The Oregonians had made a mistake. Without breaking stride I veered from their cleft to the next one, the correct one, and with no loss of face led into the Chimneys like I was born there. Pause to rope. Mr. X arrived, pale and heaving, wearing pants.

Halfway up the Chimneys we bumped against the rear of the Canadians, who had left camp (as had the Oregonians) an hour before me and 2 hours before my troops. Humiliated at being overtaken by ragged pilgrims ranging in age to the 60s, UBC youths dumped excess baggage (two exhausted girls and one loyal boy friend) and raced ahead.

Mt. Baker from Artist Point, looking across the valley of Swift Creek.

Despite everything, onto the crest of Shuksan Arm in mid-morning, half the elevation gained and a long and lovely day ahead. Rest stop at the head of the White Salmon Glacier, in a moraine below Winnie's Slide (where a Mountaineer named Winnie once slid); eat second breakfast and don crampons.

North across Nooksack valley forests, the Border Peaks, high and mighty in the morning sun. South slopes of Tomyhoi and Winchester and Goat green-inviting. Three years before we'd twice set out to climb American Border Peak but been turned back by a June storm and an August forest fire. (Someday I'd watch a fall sunset from High Pass, beneath Larrabee, and sprawl half-drunk in heather until color dimmed and Tomyhoi was a black line in milk-blue west and then come out of the trance shivering from stars.)

Well-drilled Climbing Course students cramponed rapidly up steep and hard snow of Winnie's Slide, passed through a narrow rock portal and stepped onto blue ice just where the

51

Upper Curtis Glacier rolls over the brink, spewing avalanches thousands of feet to the Lower Curtis. A few ropelengths of ice, then onto the wide shelf of Hell's Highway hanging between Summit Pyramid and valley.

A noise in the sky, an airplane circling the summit, searching. Before we left town Jim the Hawk had called me to find when we'd be on the upper slopes; he was shooting a movie of the Cascades from the air and needed scenes of climbers in action. Jim was on time but we were late. Now he found us. Supercub skimmed the crest at one end of Hell's Highway, dropped so low we ducked to dodge pontoons, then climbed-climbed-climbed, engine laboring, and barely cleared the far ridge. Several more passes and he disappeared. Too bad he'd missed his rock-climbing footage.

Plod over shadowed, icy surface, passing slipping-and-skidding kids from UBC who were not wearing crampons. Going by a girl ropeleader, an obvious veteran, I heard her lecture a novice—loud enough for old folks to hear—"*Poor* climbers tend to over-equip. This isn't the kind of place *we* use crampons." So saying, she fell on her rear. What language! What a look! What a generation gap!

At the end of Hell's Highway, the Wind Cirque, where an eddy pattern perpetually swirls a huge scoop in the snow. Several steep ropelengths. Turn the corner to the merger of the Curtis Glacier with the Sulphide Glacier, the last lap to the Summit Pyramid.

A nasty surprise. Blocking our path at a point where always before the snow had been unbroken, a crevasse 25 feet wide, upper lip 15 feet higher than the lower. Noon, now. Began to wish I'd whipped the party out of camp at 4 a.m.

Long-legged Jack to the rescue, teetering onto a precarious peninsula, leaping over emptiness and lodging with irons and ax on the far wall, clawing to the upper lip. With his belay all could follow, but slow—minutes per person, an hour for the party. Meanwhile UBC came up behind, curled lips at our clumsiness, searched for a crossing suitable for agile young experts, found none, and sat down to wait, muttering, glowering as if our Older Generation had dug the pit to spite them.

The Sulphide Plateau had been soaking up sunshine since dawn. Sink to calves in slush. Hot, windless air. My civilized party began to wilt. Some teams slowed to a half-stagger. UBC plugged swiftly by, wearing hard smiles of triumph.

Noise in the sky again, the return of the Supercub, and where had Jim been? A few passes and gone again. Where did he go?

The Plateau was long, the Pyramid a mirage in heat-hazy air. Yet after seeming-eternity leave the glacier, cross an awkward snow bridge over a moat. All that remained was a 500-foot gully scramble. But somewhere up the gully were 20-odd kids from UBC. I'd no more enter the bottom of the gully while another party was in the top—especially one that didn't like us—than stick my head in a cannon. Again I wished we'd started earlier.

Time and past time for lunch and the group could use a long rest. But it wasn't good rest; without taking a step, energy was sweated away struggling for comfort on steep, hot slabs.

I remembered the bear and wondered if he'd got down to the deep hole of Sulphide Lake. (Someday I'd visit the most enormous of Shuksan's holes, the Nooksack Cirque, beating brush on a grown-over miner's trail 2 miles, then hopping stream channels 2 more miles. From the 2500-foot floor, a dark chaos of glacial debris, look up and up 6500 feet of icefalls and cliffs.)

An hour of waiting, 2 hours. Growing feebler. Oregonians appeared on the Plateau—the first we'd seen of them since the Chimneys. A gallant try but surely they'd turn back now.

Having enjoyed an extravagant summit sackout and used up most of our afternoon, UBC streamed down the gully, smirking-certain *they* would never be as old as us. Stiff legs creaked, weary Mountaineers arose from sun-drugged sleep and entered the gully. Shortly our first teams were on the rockpile summit, admiring Baker dominant, wild Pickets close to the east, Canada near to the north, Glacier Peak far south, mountains and glaciers and forested valleys highlighted and warm in late sun. Said Dick (not Brooks), half-giggling, "This is a funny hour to be on top of Shuksan." He'd been climbing a dozen years. He knew a fiasco when he saw one.

A couple of teams were still dragging upward, half a step a minute. I should turn them back. We ought to be running, right now.

Holy names! The Supercub roared over the summit. Where had he come from?

(Later we learned where. After finding us on Hell's Highway, Jim had returned to Seattle to refuel. After finding us on the Sulphide, he was darned if he was refueling again. Circled the mountain. Spotted a dandy big lake—whether Sulphide Lake or Price Lake I don't know, and neither does Jim. Water opaque with rock milk, enclosing walls forcing a "falling-leaf" descent. Taxi alertly, dodging icebergs. Abruptly a pontoon grounded and the plane swung around. Luckily, no damage. After a proper interval to allow us to get onto rocks, the takeoff. Jim's photographer took no footage of the landing or takeoff, or even the wait on the lake. Just sat in his seat staring straight ahead.)

Now Jim got his rock-climbing scenes. Next, summit shots. Supercub roared past a hundred feet away, made a tight turn and roared back 50 feet away. Pontoons loomed close, closer. Cower behind rocks. Just my lousy luck to be a victim of the weirdest tragedy in alpine history—wiped out in a tangle of pontoons and wings, a funeral pyre of flaming gasoline. (Later, in the finished movie, I saw myself and others waving and apparently yelling enthusiastic greetings; in fact we were hysterically crying "Go away! Go away!" And worse.)

Engine stopped. Supercub hung several yards off the summit. I could feel its crushing weight. Jim stuck his head out the window and said in conversational tones, "Hey Harvey, want a ride home?" Then he went away.

Our last teams arrived, bringing news the Oregonians had entered the gully. We should be running but couldn't, not without risking first-degree mass murder. So relax. Enjoy a view forbidden to climbers who obey the rules of alpine sanity. Sun sinking westward, evening shadows in valleys, colors of forests and peaks glorious-rich. Bad things coming and nothing to be done but bask in Paradise on the brink of Hell.

Oregonians nearing the summit, out of rockfall danger. Pass them with friendly hellos but no extended parley. A quick job of the gully, and the Plateau too, everybody pushing. Then the big crevasse. During one-by-one passage the sun neared the horizon; low rays cast dramatic shadows over the glacier, too darn dramatic.

People sitting in snow, getting out crampons for the Wind Cirque. "No!" I cried. "Bellyflops! Bellyflops!" The technique saved minutes, gave hope. Run across Hell's Highway, softened since morning but now cooling. To avoid using irons, detour around ice, scramble rock pinnacles to the top of Winnie's Slide.

Sun down but western sky still creamy-blue, horizon banded scarlet and pink and yellow-green. A bare chance. "Bellyflops!" I yelled. But the Slide is longer than the Wind Cirque. Even my own team of friends objected, but even with friends I was now brutal. All teams lay on bellies and slid—standing up at the bottom to dig cold kernels from private parts and remember Winnie.

A team missing. Wait on the moraine, meanwhile sipping a delicious meltwater trickle; canteens had been exhausted for hours, we'd been eating snow by the bushel.

Missing team appeared at the top of the Slide. Ropeleader looked down the steep slope as if he'd never seen it before. Backed away from the edge, consulted with partners. Returned to the brink. Faintly came the appeal, "How—get—down?"

Shout instructions through cupped hands: "On—stomachs—arrest—position—bellyflop—glissade!"

Team listened, looked down Slide, discussed. I sensed rebellion. Leader turned and opened mouth. The words exploded from me: "YOU COME DOWN HERE *RIGHT NOW!*"

Fall back in moraine, coughing; the explosion ruptured my yelling machinery. But my voice was as a wind sweeping the laggards from feet onto bellies: I was still coughing and the party still laughing when the three arrived.

Now 8 o'clock. Sky light, peaks glowing. Beside bright glacier total dark seemed an hour away, time enough to

Price Lake and the Price Glacier, under the north wall of Mt. Shuksan.

scramble the Chimneys. Could then gain camp by flashlight. So I gave the signal to continue.

When I started down the 20-foot slab of the topmost pitch, I could see holds; when I reached the bottom, I couldn't. In those seconds solid rock melted into vagueness. Look down the upper gully of the Chimneys. Absolute night.

Said Dick (not Brooks), "I don't know about anybody else, but this is where *I'm* spending the night." Said I, "We're *all* spending the night here." Most were glad enough to call it a day, squirm some comfort from rocks. Dick (not Brooks) and his wife and I found a rubble ledge with a backrest and huddled together.

Two problems. Dick (Brooks) thought it preposterous to sit all night on the rocks and said so repeatedly, and he has a loud voice. And Mr. X could find no better roost than my personal backrest; he perched there like an ungainly bird, practically on my shoulders.

Final memory of sun left the sky. Stars in frightening numbers. No breeze, perfectly calm air. Not until 11 o'clock did I roll down shirt sleeves, put on sweater, pull stocking cap over ears, and wish I hadn't left my GI mook parka in camp. But now chill penetrated deep. Some of us dozed, some talked. Far below were bags, food—and water. If I'd called a halt on the moraine we could have filled canteens before the trickle froze. Thirsty. Shivering.

Dick (Brooks) wouldn't settle down. Roved in the dark, commenting out loud (very) on what a smart leader Manning was. He found a dribble from a snowpatch, enough for a swallow for several of us—a tantalizing dampness in the mouth. He said, chuckling, "I suppose if I left all this stupid misery without the Leader's permission that would be the same as resigning from The Mountaineers." Said I, chuckling, "That's right."

Thin rays of unseen moon flowing from behind Shuksan, dimly illumining ridges. Almost we could make out trees in the valley. Then the nearly-full moon lit the tips of pinnacles.

At somewhat past midnight Dick (Brooks) seriously wondered if I might not reconsider in the light of the moon. The light was a snare and a delusion, no real help in the shadowed Chimneys, but I was tired of this scrambling and

The Black Buttes from Mt. Baker.

kibitzing and announced permission for a maximum of four people to descend under Dick's leadership — figuring four could stick close enough together to control kicked-loose rock. Dick and Si and Long-Legged Jack were the only ones who wanted to go down who were in shape to go down. A volunteer for the number four spot—Mr. X. I was tired of having him perched on my back. Also I felt Dick deserved Mr. X.

Relax in a much quieter bivouac. Listen to rattling rock, voices calling instructions. (Plus curses; the problems Dick was facing kept up my spirits.) Then flickers of light on the trail. They were drinking water now, crawling into warm bags. Talk on, drowse on, dry-mouthed, shivering.

Moon had washed out the brilliance of stars, given peaks and valleys and bivouac soft-glimmering mystery. Now dawnlight overwhelmed moonlight, restoring harsh reality. Boulders and slabs formed from black void. At 5 a.m., arise to creaking, snapping, crackling of joints and begin the descent. At 8 a.m., stagger on rickety legs into the heather bedroom I had left, alone, 26 hours before.

Dick (Brooks) greeted me with a pot of punch. Drain the pot and crawl into the shadow of a boulder—to avoid the sun! Who would have thought, high on dark rocks just 3 hours before, the world could be too warm?

Awake at noon. Quiet meadows. My people had broken camp and hiked out. The UBC youths had left in early morning. The Oregonians had arrived after a bivouac at the top of Winnie's Slide and continued straight home to Oregon.

No longer a loud-mouthed Leader. Just an anarchist. (The next year the Climbing Committee reverted to a 2-day ascent of Shuksan, declaring Manning had proved the peak was too difficult for 3 days.)

A supper missed, a breakfast missed, but not hungry. Just thirsty. Dick and I sat in the shade of a huge block of rock fallen from Shuksan Arm, next to a creek pouring through green grass and soft heather, over a tiny falls into a bubble-sparkling pool.

(Two summers later Betty and I would come to this same shadow, this same pool, with Penny, 4½, and Becky, 3. The summer was hot, the week was hot, and all streams from Austin Pass to camp were too warm for ideal drinking. Incredibly, Lake Anne was comfortable for wading and swimming. Only this one spring-fed creek was as cold as mountain water should be, and only this one boulder gave deep shade. A memorable family trip. Our strange puppy with the piebald eyes, Tasha the Terror of Marmots, turned up her nose at dogfood; we worried until we found she was grazing night and day on blueberries—and how did she learn they were good to eat? And Penny and I, on a granite talus, watched two weasels chase a conie in and out of crevices under our feet. And below Austin Pass on the way home, hot-and-bothered Becky was stung by a yellowjacket and howled and wept and refused to go on until the Universe apologized.)

By the clear cool pool Dick and I began to drink. Mix a pot of purple punch and drink that. Mix a pot of orange punch and drink that. Mix a pot of chocolate milk and drink that. Mix leftover powdered milk and drink that. Sack it for hours in the shade of the big block of rock, drinking. And looking to Summit Pyramid, Wind Cirque, Hell's Highway, Fischer Chimneys, bivouac.

A Closeup of the Black Buttes.

CHAPTER 6

Luna Cirque

At first gray light in dank forest the Rover Boys began waking up the birds. I burrowed deeper in the bag to escape, hating Rover Erick, Rover Paul, and Rover Bob and stuck with them for a week. Worse, the other five, though properly somber for the hour and weather, accepted the idiot cheerfulness as a call to awake. Even my buddy Ray ("The Avalanche That Walks Like a Man") scratched and yawned.

Rovers hollered around the woods. Next to my ear Ray crunched Grape Nuts like a concrete mixer. Then Climbing Chairman Vic was standing over me saying, "Everybody's ready to go. Aren't you going to get up?" My eight comrades of the 1950 Climbers Outing were fed, booted, packed, and hot to walk—and it wasn't yet 7 o'clock, the best sleep still ahead.

I spoke not to Vic, to no person specifically, but informed the gloomy, dripping Chilliwack valley and anyone who might be listening that this was a hiking day and hikers keep more civilized hours than climbers. Silence was my answer—silence, snickers, and twitches. Social pressure drove me from the sack. At 7:30.

The trip was doomed. I'd felt it before we left town, which I didn't want to leave, being sated with summits after a strenuous spring and summer and not sure I even liked mountains anymore; the reason I finally came along was the previous winter I'd fought for the Pickets when most of the Climb-

The Luna Cirque, looking from slopes of Mt. Challenger to Mt. Fury.

ing Committee, not too sure where or what the Pickets were, wanted to schedule the outing amid more famous peaks: came July and Chairman Vic reminded me.

The day before, driving up Ruth Creek, one of our two cars made a wrong turn and spent 3 hours in a mudhole. When we finally took up burdens the afternoon was late. At Hannegan Pass, cold fog blowing. The sun would never shine again.

Now morning clouds were low and thick and trees were tall and decrepit and drippy and the Chilliwack trail fell toward nowhere. Stop for the first rest, still too early for rational hikers to be awake. I slipped free from packstraps and the rucksack tied atop packboard slipped free from lashings, fell 20 feet, bounced, flew through a waterfall and splatted and splashed another 50 feet. If a Rover had so much as smirked I'd have skulled him with my ax. Down mossy slabs and mud and thorns to the cliff bottom, retrieve sack from plunge-basin. The jam jar had busted; crampons and pitons and carabiners and slings were gooey with strawberry slime. Worse, the toilet roll was water-saturated to the core. Bad moments to look forward to. The trip was doomed.

Down, down the Chilliwack. Glimpses from forest of trees marching up valley walls into clouds. Out of woods briefly into smothering bracken fern and slashing sticker-bushes, using the extra 70 pounds of the stone on my back to juggernaut through, clumsy and mindless as Dr. Frankenstein's maltreated monster. Here, at least, a view north out the glacier-carved Chilliwack valley to Canada—more wild, ancient trees, more clouds.

At the Brush Creek turnoff, cross the Chilliwack River on a log. The first good news. The Forest Service hadn't sent a trail crew within miles of the Pickets since pre-war CCC days and we were prepared for a lousy alder-busting afternoon. But the U.S. Geological Survey was on the scene, running a ground-control line for what would be the first accurate map of the area. By necessity, not choice, cartographers and surveyors had re-opened the trail from the Skagit to the Chilliwack. The cook, in camp by the crossing, said that while fishing the Little Beaver he'd seen lots of bear. Most were black but one was a silvertip grizzly. That's what he said.

Tapto Shelter was the next good news. Not because it offered shelter—four or five guys might sleep inside if they were very good friends—but because that was our day's destination and we wouldn't have to torture our backs anymore.

Dropping 70 pounds gives a moon-like release, turns a plodding walker into a light-bodied leaper. The 11 miles and 8 hours of hauling the stone had softened every muscle, but after supper feet barely had to touch the trail to send me flying through subalpine trees and heather.

Not that I flew. Could if I wanted, even in meltwater muck, but didn't want. Better in evening to bounce slowly away and alone from Rover racket. Now I was 16 miles from the cars, in wild country with silvertip grizzlies, even. And the solid sheet of clouds was thinning to white wisps. Above, Whatcom Peak. Snowfields (or were they glaciers?) and cliffs and ridges showed no walk-up route. And it was only 7574 feet high, a humble neighbor of the Pickets. What would the *real* Pickets be like?

Next dawn Rovers screamed and hollered and giggled and I damned them but the five others lept to attention and one last time I argued and lost and at 7:15 we were on the up-trail together. Air chill, sky blue. In a mile, sunshine at mile-high Whatcom Pass. Brush Creek behind, steep-sided, avalanche-torn valley of the Little Beaver before, far sharp horn of Hozomeen on the horizon beyond the Skagit. Here, 17 miles from road-end, leave trail. A few yards of heather, a screen of alpine fir, and the white explosion of the Challenger Glacier.

Bad weather over, 17 miles of trail behind, peaks ahead. Packs seemed lighter as we traversed meadows and scree and buttresses and snowfields (or was it a glacier?) on the east side of Whatcom Peak. Vic pointed to what appeared to be

Traversing from Whatcom Pass toward Whatcom Peak.

a crevasse and wondered, "Do you think we should rope up?" Impatient to get on, feeling immortal, I said, "Hell no, it's just a hole in the snow."

An island of polished slabs, stop for lunch. Beneath, the lower tongue of the Challenger, fed by ice tumbling down cliffs from the upper glacier; several avalanches rumbled as we ate. An oddity in the lower tongue—a wide, deep hole ringed by concentric crevasses, as if the bottom of the glacier was falling out.

A last mile around the corner of Whatcom. Then heather and ice-scratched buttresses and lichen-covered boulders and snow-melt pools of perfectly-named Perfect Pass. East, right next to camp, a cornice poised above the glacier. West, cliffs falling to Mineral Creek, a headwater of the Baker River. South, tomorrow's mountain, Challenger.

North, an easy 1700 feet of snow rose to Whatcom Peak. Saying nothing to anyone, at 3:05 I began kicking steps. This was what the last 3 days were for. Noticing what I was doing the gang fell in behind. Halfway to the top, the slope steepening, Erick realized he'd forgotten his ax and went flying to camp and caught us just before we reached the summit at 4 o'clock.

Challenger hid the other Pickets except for the eastern outrigger, Luna, but we could see south to Triumph, Despair, Glacier Peak on the far horizon, and even Three Fingers and Whitehorse, standing over Puget Sound lowlands. Above Easy Ridge to the west, enormous Shuksan, from whose summit I'd first seen the Pickets 2 years earlier; behind it, the whitest volcano of them all, Baker. North were the massive and rugged Chilliwack peaks, 8956-foot Redoubt and 8976-foot Glacier (later re-named Spickard). East, range on range to and beyond the Skagit. The trip wasn't doomed after all.

Fast standing glissades down mushy suncups, trailing clouds of churned-up snow. A cluck-clucking mother ptarmigan tried to decoy us from camp. But her pinfeather-sprouting chick (just one) was feeling too old and bold for the freeze-in-the-heather act. He dove off a buttress, flapping spindly wings and dropping like a rock, mother going cluck-cluck-*cluck*. Was this how she lost the rest of her brood? After a while he re-appeared, *walking* up the hill.

From a nest under a clump of tight-limbed midget firs, watch the sun dip behind Shuksan, glaciers of Baker glow pink. Now 20 walking miles and 3 days deep in wildness and nowhere was mankind (except us) to be seen or heard. To sleep, content.

Shivering from cold air outside and hot cocoa inside, watch the sun reach over still-dark Cascades to light the summits of Shuksan and Baker. Laugh, Rovers! At 6:30, no murmur of objection from me, up and away, crunching boots into night-frozen snow, headed toward the first big challenge. Weave through crevasses, cat-step over snow bridges, traverse the Challenger Glacier 2 miles to the snow ridge separating Little Beaver drainage from Luna Creek. Drop loads, stow rucksacks, eat second breakfast (first lunch). Then upward, half-stunned by the first glimpse of Luna Cirque.

So much elevation went fast and easy, a simple snow hike to within a few hundred feet of the summit, I was disappointed. Challenger? Where was the challenge? Here—the bergschrund, the upper lip 50 feet above the lower—that's where. We'll have some fun after all. Explore back and forth looking for a route. No route, or at least no easy way. No way except one. And no fun there.

Roy and I seemed to be elected to lead, though damned if I remember a vote. The slope we'd have to climb was around the corner from the schrund, steep and exposed, falling to a far-below jumble of seracs. Because our boot-soles were the new-fashion rubber lugs just becoming popular, we'd have to wear crampons. But within the past week (today was August 1) a heavy snowfall had covered the underlying corn with 4 inches of stocky slush, the sort of stuff that balls crampons into spherical skates.

Lashing on irons, feeling serious. Suddenly Vic announces *he'd* like to lead. Exhale. Agree with all my heart his old-fashioned tricouni-nailed boots are better weapons for the situation.

Vic walks delicately along the knife-ridge lower lip of the bergschrund. Belayed by Bob, crosses a bridge built more of air than snow, chops toeholds and handholds up a 15-foot wall, then throws a leg over the corner and commits himself to the final slope. Under him, emptiness; in a fall, Bob's belay at most would provide a line for retrieving broken remains.

Jamming ax deep, kicking boots through slush to gain purchase in corn, standing vertical, moving smoothly, he runs out the rope—and still is not on top. Bob is forced to abandon his belay and follow. Now both are committed. One slip by either and both are lost. A few more hard-swinging, sweating steps and Vic is on the flat and the whole party is safe. Exhale.

A wind scoop, a snow ridge, then the summit tower. "Your turn," says Vic. Start up the rock, easy scrambling, no pain. But a considerable volume of air under my heels. Banging in a peg would solve inner tensions, only I left strawberry-sticky ironware below. Retreat to Roy's belay and borrow his pitons and carabiners and hammer, return upward, engineer an anchor and squirm over the exposed edge to a table. My 10 pounds of iron, carried over 22 miles of trail and glacier, were never used.

The register was interesting. In 1936, 14 years before, the first ascent by Dickert, Hossack, and McGowan. In 1940 the Beckey brothers and a Ptarmigan party signed the book, and in 1949, Bengtson, Misch, and Powers. We were fifth. And impressed to follow in the tracks of men who had been our teachers and heros.

The view included all we had seen from Whatcom. But now also Luna Cirque and Crooked Thumb, Phantom, and Fury—the roughest, toughest ice and rock in our group experience. Were we really in the Cascades?

Getting so large a party up and down the schrund and summit tower made a long day. Blistered and thirsty to packs at 6 o'clock, rest, and plunge-step. We'd planned to camp at Luna Lake, on the far side of the cirque, but at 7 p.m. came to snow-free ground on Challenger Arm and were satisfied.

Our split-level camp hung in the air on narrow heather ledges, each big enough for one or two climbers. (The Rovers found a three-man perch.) Ledges were already in shadow when we arrived. Evening wind steady and cold; any gear not anchored blew off and away and down, down, down.

The ragged summit line ran from 8236-foot Challenger to 8292-foot Fury, Crooked Thumb and Phantom and nameless pinnacles between. The wall hypnotized: 4000 vertical feet of

Summit pitch of Mt. Challenger.

hanging glaciers and rock faces and ribs dropping to the dark, rough floor of the cirque.

I remembered the South Pole entry in Scott's journal: "Good God, what an awful place." We were 6 miles of glacier and snow and scrambles from the trail, 23 walking miles from the cars. Scott didn't make it all the way back from *his* trip. In case of trouble, how long before we could summon help? At least 4 days, I reckoned. We nine were on our own near the "pole of remoteness" of the Cascades.

The great wall lived. Hear a loud rumble, pivot quickly and scan high origins of the sound, see nothing. Then spot moving rubble down low, fanning over a dirty avalanche cone. Turn your back on the wall and you'll miss the show. So sit and stare, rove over patches of fractured ice and wonder how they stick to such steep ribs. Now—there it goes, a white torrent pouring silently over a cliff, spraying a snowfield, spewing over another cliff—and finally comes the roar. Day and night, every few minutes, somewhere on the wall something moved, something crashed, rumbled, roared

Swimming in Perfect Lake.

Fury stayed bright longest, light streaming from the west onto upper snows and rocks. Then all the peaks etched black against sunset pink. Wrapped cosily alone in tarp, snuggled in soft heather nook, lying on my back, nothing between me and sky and peaks. Chew a bed-time Mars bar, watching summits dim, setting moon red as a dying sun, then stars one by one, cluster by cluster. And sleep.

We decided to recuperate from the psychic strain of Challenger before trying Fury. Luna was our rest-day objective, a walk-up, a hike. The Rovers didn't start chattering until 7 o'clock. I was already awake. Who could sleep, confronted by the wall?

By now the Rovers and I were friends; I had learned to tolerate their unnatural dawn happiness and they had learned not to come within 25 feet of me before I finished my morning cocoa and fig bar. We taught each other much. I found there is no savage utterly lacking possibilities of humanity. Erick told me— much later— he didn't fully appreciate the wall until he watched me watch it.

Morning sun warmed camp, chased out dark fears. Who said this was an "awful place"? Wall vivid-bright and noisier than ever, a wall of strength and joy.

Relaxed breakfast in cloudy morning. At 11 o'clock begin the rest-day romp. Traverse a mile closer to the cirque headwall over snow and scree and scraps of meadow, in and out gullies. Skate down avalanche fans to the cirque floor, losing 1500 feet—a poor way to start a climb.

Crossing the floor cooled our holiday spirit. From above we'd admired the classic arcuate form of the terminal moraine. Now we scrambled up and down its steep, loose gravel, and up and down again, and up and down smaller and non-classic heaps of trash we hadn't noticed from above. Summits were messy with clouds but the sun was still hot for gravel-staggering.

At last, garbage conquered. Climb honest snow 1000 feet to Luna Lake. What lake? Merely a flat white patch streaked with lines of melting-out blue. Stare up an icefall and a steep couloir, the route to Fury—hard to believe. But that was tomorrow's problem. Today's problem was 3500 more feet on snow sloppy in scorching sun, then a gneiss felsenmeer radiating heat like a stovelid. Where were clouds now we needed them? Thick and picturesque in the west, but burned away from our rest-day hell.

On the summit of 8285-foot Luna, all forgiven. Look as before into Luna Cirque and the Northern Pickets, the Fury Group. But now, too, look into McMillan Cirque and the Southern Pickets, the Terror Group. All the Pickets strung in a line. Was this the Cascades for sure?

The register said Ptarmigans Cox and Thompson had been here in 1938, followed in 1940 by the Beckey brothers and more Ptarmigans. We were fourth. To the best of our knowledge, gained from summit books and climbing journals, ours was only the sixth party to climb anywhere in the Northern Pickets—12 people before us, and now our 9-man population explosion.

Look to camp across the deeps of Luna Cirque, on faraway slopes of Challenger Arm. Eat kipper snacks and Sailor Boy pilot bread. Dream of being over there, sacked out in a heather bed drinking a pot of lemonade.

Gaining and losing 6000 feet (or was it 7000, counting the moraines?) isn't too tough a job—except maybe for a rest day when you don't start walking much before noon. Even the rough upsy-downsy of the cirque floor (twice) wouldn't have done in our morale. It was the way the itinerary was arranged to conclude with that bumble-footed pratfalling struggle over moraines dark in shadow of the again-ominous wall, and that 1500-foot slog out of the hole.

Plug steps up evening-frozen snow, listening to rumbles of avalanches and empty stomachs. Too tired to plug. So rest. (" 'Tis cold, 'tis bitter cold, and I am sick at heart.") Plug on, destroying human flesh muscle by muscle, cell by cell.

I was in the lead when my brain disintegrated. Glance over shoulder. Nobody laughing, nobody saw the joke, not even the Rovers. All were grim machines, head down, staring at boot heels. I tried them out with eccentric variations on the normal zig-zag monotony: zig 40 steps left, zag only 3 steps right, zig 3 left and zag 40 right. All eyes stared down, no flicker of intelligence. Though cracked, mine was the only functioning mind. The others were the tail on my kite, following every crazy whim. Put them to the final test. Ease the angle over, and over, and over more, and kick steps downhill, back into the cirque. Only after several machines started down in my tracks did a low moan arise, swelling to a general groan of agony and loathing. Thus my revenge for Rover mornings and bad moments with mushy toilet paper.

At 8, flop on heather pads. Ray's turn as party cook. He managed to get water hot enough over a gust-driven fire of twigs to make a pot of sticky potatoes flavored with salami that had left the butcher shop a week before. The kind of meal one remembers through the night.

While eating in twilight we talked about tomorrow, the Fury day. I renounced my share of glory. I wanted a rest day to recuperate from the rest day and planned to wander ice-scrubbed rocks toward Phantom, absorbing more of the wall and perhaps taking a shower in a certain magical waterfall. After that, loiter up snows to the easy 7374-foot peak above camp to the east. (I kept my date with that peak 18 years later. We hiked the Little Beaver from Ross Lake to Beaver Pass, left trail and beat steeply up forests to meadows, explored peaklets and basinlets and frozen lakes of Challenger Ridge, and came to the peak. Look across glacier to the splinter summit of Challenger. Down to the site of what had been, in 1950, the lower tongue of the glacier; the tongue was entirely gone and where the odd hole had been, a gray-green lake now. Over to slopes of Whatcom,

where in 1950 we wondered if we were on snowfield or glacier; an impassable icefall now. And also look down to the "awful place" of the 1950 camp. And stare again at the living wall.)

Several others also had private plans. But Fury still had five. Parka hoods over heads against wind, chewing rotten salami and burping, barely able to stand, they were ready to face—for openers—another round-trip to Luna Lake. Scott was not the last of the heroes.

There wasn't any morning. At the hour when Rovers should have been blaspheming the dawn peace, 16 other eyes opened with mine and saw the low ceiling of swift clouds sweeping the crest of Fury. Things could be worse. If we'd been faster on Challenger we might now be camped at Luna Lake.

In dull non-morning the separate camps stirred. I crunched Grape Nuts and drank cocoa and ate a fig bar, watching the wall. On their three-man bench close above my shelf, Rovers mumbled low, playing breakfast games in the wind with a cranky primus stove. Fury was out of the question. Heroism, though, might demand our sticking out the storm in hopes of

Air view of Mt. Fury and the Luna Cirque.

a quick recovery. Only Thursday and we weren't due home until Sunday.

A short, bitter blizzard. Totally convincing. At 11 we began the retreat, humbly aware how far it was, how very very far, to trees. Big heavy packs on backs. Plug steps, bracing against wind, soaking up slashing rain and flurries of snow and sleet. The Pickets didn't want us.

Tapto Shelter at 5 p.m. Old home. Lord, what a marvel are trees! After days of sterile white snow and gray rock, wrap mortal flesh in a luxury of green life. The storm wasn't a really hard blow after all—but how would it be, just now, on the heather ledges of Awful Camp?

The umbilical cord of trail led securely homeward. A long walk, down and up and down, but safe every step. On Friday, the sky somewhat clearing but perhaps still storming on Fury, descend into grand wild forests. After heather and alpine scrub, what huge plants seemed the trees. A greater mystery than glaciers.

A side-trail into high country west of the Chilliwack. Have to walk that sometime. (And 18 years later I did, with the entire Manning Gang plus Ira the Spring. A homecoming trip, roaming meadows of Copper Mountain, gazing over green deeps of the Chilliwack to Perfect Pass, Whatcom Peak, Challenger Glacier,

On the Challenger Glacier, looking to Perfect Pass and Whatcom Peak, Mt. Shuksan in the distance.

Luna Peak, all the Fury Group, and remembering 1950 and telling kids how it was in the Olden Days before they were born. A homecoming trip in another way, too, because the full family was along, including 15-year-old Penny, so ill and crippled in 1967 we had no week-long high-country family outing that summer and didn't know if there'd ever be another and now she was glissading the hell out of the snowfield above our basecamp at frozen Egg Lake.)

The final camp at Hannegan Pass. After a crummy dinner, all nine sprawled on the ground, me tossing left-over Sailor Boy to a beggar doe. Vic yells, "Why not throw some of that *our* way?" So I sail discs of pilot bread and feed my friends. (Next day we invaded a tiny restaurant in the hamlet of Glacier and ordered nine hamburger steaks, nine quarts of milk, and nine slices of apple pie a-la-mode; we first frightened the proprietors with the size of our order—they had to round up the total resources of the town to satisfy our lust for milk—and then terrified them with our animal attack on the food.)

Cloudy and threatening Saturday. Run loose-legged to the Ruth Creek road. The cheery U.S. Geological Survey cook served us coffee on the trail; we listened to his radio, with news of the disaster in Korea. Strange after the Pickets there could still be a Korea. Stranger after Luna Cirque that voices could speak from a box. Strangest of all, after days of hiking, to sit in a car and watch trees whiz by at a dizzy 10 miles an hour.

The Manning Gang backpacking through suncups on the ridge of Copper
Mountain, Mt. Shuksan in background.

CHAPTER 7

Running The Eastern Ridges

Sleep by the way. In morning, up the Methow valley, sagebrush-and-scabrock hills, green ravines. Where the North Cross-State Highway (under construction) turns left to Early Winters Creek and Washington Pass, continue straight past hay ranches into forests. Climb and climb switchbacks, pausing to look out the U-shaped trough of the ancient Methow Glacier. Around Dead Horse Point. (Before the road was blasted, many pack animals didn't make the precipice corner and fell to Rattlesnake Creek, far down.) Now parkland. At 6198 feet, Harts Pass. A spur road north, nearly to the 7440-foot summit of Slate Peak, the main road descending Slate Creek to ghost towns of Barron and Chancellor and a dead-end.

Old country, this. Before the turn of the century thousands of "dirty miners" clawed and scratched "in search of shining gold." Owen Wister, whose novel, *The Virginian*, derived from people he knew and anecdotes he heard during his stay in the Methow, crossed Harts Pass by packtrain on a honeymoon visit to Puget Sound.

Being able to drive to 6000 feet allows a short-legged family party a maximum of high walking on a weekend. Take the trail north, contouring Japanese-style rock gardens on Slate Peak. A drink of cold water in Benson Basin, a shoulder topped by a frail lone larch that demands an against-the-sky photograph, then the wide swale of Windy Pass at the head of Barron Basin. Below east, the West Fork Pasayten River; beyond, cirque-pocked ridges of Pasayten wildlands, some of the lonesomest country in the West.

A viper in Eden. Miners (I can think of a better name) have scarred Barron Basin with bulldozers, blasted pits in green lawns, scattered garbage and junk lumber, gulled greedy nitwits into buying thousands of shares of stock. Tonnage of ore extracted, close to zero. Under terms of the 1872 Mining Act, no matter: frontier fraudulence, frontier foolishness, have full freedom of these hills, in 1969 as in 1872.

To save sanity, put the desecration out of mind—temporarily, pending bitter letters to Senators and Congressmen. Climb above barbarism, scramble lazy and slow by splashing creeks, heather and clean scree, to the table top of 7400-foot Tamarack Peak. Relax. Look west to the close bulk of 8928-foot Jack, king of the Skagit. And south to giant Ballard and Azurite, well above 8000. And east to Pasayten ridges. And north to Canada. Rotate for hours.

After a few years of gazing north along the Cascade Crest and never getting farther than Tamarack, Dick and I began to feel frustrated. No peaks up there worth bagging, but that wasn't

Climbers are terrible snobs. I used to look east from rough, cold summits of the Pickets and Chilliwacks to rounded ranges beyond Ross Lake and express profound contempt in borrowed German: "nein gletscher, nein gipfel." None of my friends had ever been there and the climber's bible, *Beckey's Guide*, tossed off whole rows of 8000-foot mountains with a bored sentence or two apiece. Probably good enough for Boy Scouts and horses, I thought.

Then one Fourth-of-July weekend Dick Brooks decided to see if Harts Pass was a total loss. I'd just returned from a financially-compulsory tour of American cities and was in no shape for climbing, and about over the hill anyway, and went along for the ride. Small expectations and therefore all the greater the amazement. We felt a poignant sense of homecoming—it was rambling Olympic ridges much like these, on Boy Scout hikes from Camp Parsons, we'd begun our pre-climber high-country lives.

The trip became a Brooks and Manning family favorite for the Fourth, a time of summer when peaks west are still mostly white but the thinner snowpack in their lee is dwindling to patches, meadows are greening, larches sprouting new needles.

Drive in evening over Snoqualmie Pass and Swauk Pass, down the Wenatchee valley to the Columbia, up the once-mighty, now-ponded "River of the West." Over a sagebrush ridge to Lake Chelan, fond twilight views of the water-road mountains.

One small corner of the vast Horseshoe Basin tundra; beyond, Windy Peak.

our game anymore. New country. Surprises. A vast province of unknown Cascades.

We tried a flank attack by way of Canada, the head of Ross Lake, and the trail over Willow Pass to Lightning Creek and the Freezeout. Much peaceful rain sleep beside a stream, drops drifting between water-heavy branches of firs and hemlocks. Tantalizing meadows above in fog. A splendid rain-and-forest hike, but we nourished a grudge: "Remember the Freezeout!"

In September 1966 Dick and I came to Harts Pass equipped for a week-long sally north; since we'd have to retrace steps, chances were small of settling scores with the Freezeout, but we'd have a go.

Or rather, a fiasco. Weather lousy. Impossible to lift 50-pound packs in hard rain sweeping the ridges. And worst, this was the opening weekend of the "high country hunt," when all over the Cascades campground deer tamed by a summer-long acquaintance with humans are fatally disillusioned.

Mope around the pass, not allowed to enjoy the somber gray peace of drizzle and mist, not with steady bang-bang-bang, constant encounters with hard-eyed gunmen; sure no time to step in the bushes for a moment of privacy. The warfare actually was being conducted against beer cans, whiskey bottles, birds, and chipmunks; all the pet deer had met their doom by dawn of opening day. To us, the only pacifists among a hundred warriors, the sport seemed as exciting as machine-gunning dairy cows in a pasture. To each his own, to each his own.

Another poor morning deepened funk. A cheerful idiot who had been razzing up and down roads all weekend on his brand new toy motorcycle told us 75 cavalrymen plus support troops were picketed north of Harts Pass. The presence of 75 guns, 100 or more horses, and a month's output of a Kentucky distillery ruined our enthusiasm.

Blocked north. Yet a new section of Cascade Crest Trail had just been built south—to where? Monday the weather cleared. Hoist packs and set off south to see.

Plenty to see. On frost-cracked boulders of Mt. Hardy, Dick recalled a confrontation with a Forest Service apologist, arguing

Abandoned miner's cabin in the ghost town of Chancellor.

about a North Cascades National Park then nothing but a dream, being told of this area, "It's not National Park caliber." Looking down Swamp Creek to Granite Creek, route of the now-abuilding North Cross-State Highway, and to enormous Black Peak, oddly cross-lighted by evening sunrays slipping under storm clouds, Dick said bitterly, "Definitely not National Park caliber!"

On a grim-cold afternoon with swift clouds sheeting from the west, we explored pink granodiorite beneath Golden Horn and Tower Mountain into the basin of Snowy Lakes Pass. Larches yellowing for autumn. Meadows dying in a violence of final color. Gather memories to sustain the spirit in months of darkness. By shores of a rock-set tarn, I decided if this weren't part of Heaven, when my time came I wouldn't go. Dick murmured, "No, not National Park caliber."

Far north, the Freezeout remained unknown. An unbearable mystery. Winter and spring discussions of strategy. Then a few days before a vacation week began and we had to go somewhere, Dick's brother Burt agreed to come along, a welcome addition to party strength and sociability. And a friend of Dick's, a Methow native, offered to drop us at Harts Pass. And the Brooks Wives volunteered to collect us at Diablo Dam. The complete blueprint.

Saturday night, July 29, at Windy Pass, 4 miles from Harts Pass. Light lingered oddly late in the sky north. A strange flash on the Arctic horizon. Another. Dancing, flickering beams. Coyotes barked under the Northern Lights. Cold breeze grew to a semi-gale, tore the campfire to streamers of flying sparks, drove us to sacks in clumps of alpine fir.

Sunday morning a patchy, slow-moving, probably harmless cloud ceiling. Leave scars of marauding mine-share promoters and jeep-riding, scooter-riding hunters. Enter the North Cascade Primitive Area (now the Pasayten Wilderness Area), closed to motorized vehicles.

High walking, views west and east, on and near the Cascade Crest: Windy Basin, Oregon Basin, Foggy Pass, Jim Pass, and down to 5150-foot Holman Pass—lowest Crest elevation from Canada to far south of Harts Pass. Upward through forest in afternoon, past conglomerate cliffs; after 11 backpacking miles, parkland of Goat Lakes Camp. Late sun streaming down meadows in the headwater basin of Canyon Creek. Each alpine tree a green glow and a black shadow.

In this paradise, a slum—cavalry headquarters for the "high-country hunt." Meadows stomped to sterile brown dirt. Generations-old alpine trees logged by ax and saw to build corrals and stoke whiskey-roaring he-man campfires. Tons of junk stoves, rotten pack boxes, rusty nails, moldy burlap, cracked plastic sheets, broken tools, empty bottles, horse crap. The garbage home of men with garbage souls.

Away from it all in morning, over and down a green roll to Lower Goat Lake, enclosed by meadow-marsh and subalpine forest. Then up beside a noisy cataract to a quiet snow-filled slot and into the secret basin of Upper Goat Lake. Blossoms and ice-scratched slabs at water's edge. Ice-rounded buttresses of conglomerate at cirque rim. Blue sky and white clouds seen through a screen of soft-needled, wind-waving larch.

Climb grass and flowers to flat meadows of filled-in lakes, to waterfalls, to bouldery heather whistling with marmots, to raw moraine, to suncupped snow, to sky-surrounded ridge.

Gulp near and far views. Stare hard in desperate joy, storing a cud of memories for winter chewing.

The ridge above Goat Lakes, storm-and-glacier country west, sunshine-and-ridge country east, set the pattern of the gulp-and-run week, bombarded day after day by totally-new barrages of high and low glory, stunned into dream-walking. Awake each morning excited. Sack out each night full—and anticipating tomorrow.

A week—a summer—would have been too short for Goat Lakes and the headwater highlands of Canyon Creek. But the Brooks Wives would be waiting at week's end somewhere below peaks now distant in the west. Tear away in afternoon, backpack 2½ miles over Rock Pass to snowfields of Coney Basin. Camp 3 in carpets of heather, clumps of larch and fir, ice-shaped buttresses. Clear sky, meteors of the Perseid Shower. Cold night-wind. Coyotes barking.

Tiffany Mountain, near the high road from the Methow to the Okanogan. On the 8000-foot summit, long views west to glaciered peaks of the main ranges of the Cascades.

To Woody Pass Tuesday, around Three Fools Peak, above Mountain Home Basin, up and up to the 7400-foot summit of Lakeview Ridge, highest point on the entire Cascade Crest Trail from the Columbia to Canada. So much air—valleys east, valleys west, infinite sky. Western peaks of Chilliwacks and Pickets blinding-white, eastern ridges burning-brown. Forests below, rivers within trees; listen, thirsty, to unattainable cold water running. Late in afternoon, away from horizons to the cirque of Hopkins Lake.

Through Hopkins Pass Wednesday and along a wooded side-hill to 5250-foot Castle Pass. Here, 27 miles from Harts Pass, the new-style 4-foot-wide, 10 per cent grade Cascade Crest Trail leaves the Cascade Crest and descends Route Creek to Canada. Our way was westward, remaining on the Crest, on the old-style Three Fools trail built by boots and hooves in a long-ago age innocent of dynamite. The sketchy track climbed a thousand feet, then followed ups and downs of the Crest. After a 9½-mile day, Camp 5, nearly 7000 feet, in a ridge-top meadow

between Big Face Creek and Castle Creek. Water supply, a snow-field. Views far southeast to country we'd walked, west to country we'd be walking.

In sunset, flashes on a forested ridge north. At night, flickers of light. A mystery—and a shock: these were *automobiles* on the Trans-Canada Highway. We'd penetrated deeper into wilderness for days, coming to feel (though knowing better) the trail might continue wilder and wilder to the Arctic. But now we'd almost come out the other side. And that evening the SAS polar jet flew above, minutes from Seattle, hours from Europe. Earth is small, wilderness smaller yet.

Thursday morning, down a steep meadow violent red with Indian paintbrush. At Big Face Creek drop packs and climb avalanche-swept grasslands under the "big face" of Joker Mountain, into a high basin of waterfalls and moss and blossoms. A lonely place. Miles from trail, and that trail rarely traveled. Few people have been in Big Face Basin. Again, a week, a summer, would not be enough.

Moraine and snow to the col. Below, a blue-green lake flecked with floating ice, rimmed by cliffs and scree and snow. An end of the grudge: this was a source of the Freezeout. Secrets remained around the corner of Blizzard Peak, but now we'd known the Freezeout not only from low down in rain but from on high in sun.

Down in shivering shadows, leaving the Cascade Crest which here trends north to Canada. Camp 6 on a tiny gravel island in Big Face Creek. Loud and plentiful water. Dippers bouncing at the knees on boulders next to the campfire.

Friday, climb 2000 steep feet through forest, avalanche green-ery, meadows again, and again a high crest. After such a full week, could more be absorbed without madness? Elbow Basin parklands, a silver ribbon meandering amid groves of alpine trees. A semicircle of green ridges, meadows made for running. Another week demanded here—and why isn't Elbow Basin long-since famous? Dream-walking to Camp 7 in a grassy saddle between the basin and the Freezeout. Water from snowfield drips. Firewood from a clump of huddled trees.

A week walking deeper into strangeness. This evening, reality lost. Queer, trembling light of setting sun. Grass glowing gold. Blossoms of red heather, white heather. A porcupine waddling into alpine scrub and flaring rear-end quills.

Ridges of Cascade Crest and Pasayten receding east in night. South, new views of peaks become familiar hiking the Crest. Below north, shadows invading Freezeout forests of our rain camp. West, the Pickets now near across the air mass of the drowned Skagit River. The sun fell behind twin summits of Hozo-meen, blinding rays flaring from dark towers. Looming over Hopkins Lake east, old Camp 4, a cumulonimbus brown and black. But no fear. No tarp. To bed under stars, drugged. Our last high night, our final high ridge. Tomorrow, the end.

No hurry to leave, Saturday morning. How long had we been high? Difficult to remember lowlands. Could we ever come down after being this high this long?

Slowly down. The trail touched the ridge above Freezeout Lake, wind-ruffled sun-glinting waters, green shores. A silver forest cost an hour and many dollars in camera film.

A fast drop down a burn meadow, south-facing, waterless, dusty. Slower, pausing to rest knees, down and down in thin and worthless shade of scrubby trees. Throat dusty, knees floppy as a rag doll. And down and down and down, 4000 steep dry feet down into forest, discovering why Elbow Basin isn't famous. At last Three Fools Creek, the first large river of the week, an entire river full of water, all ours. Duck head in a green-transparent pool, the first drink since Elbow Ridge. Sit on a rock with bare feet in riffles. After days of looking down from summits to valleys, look up from the bright river avenue. Tall trees. Meadows and ridges impossibly far above.

Long lunch rest, and then up packs for a several-hour stroll to Ross Lake—or so we expected. During afternoon and early evening we learned another reason Elbow Basin isn't famous. Why couldn't the trail follow the water grade? Because Three Fools Creek runs in a deep, steep gorge and the trail pre-dates dynamite, climbing high over tops of cliffs, dropping low under feet of cliffs, climbing again, dropping again. Three Fools Creek joined Lightning Creek and Three Fools trail intersected Lightning trail, a much more important thoroughfare; hopes now of a final simple downhill. But Lightning Creek flows in an even deeper, steeper gorge and still no dynamite; up and down again, up and down, we three fools.

Nearly 7 p.m. Almost 14 miles walked, many thousands of feet lost but thousands regained and lost again. The trail swung out of the Lightning gorge onto west-facing pine slopes, cliffy and brown-grassy, reminding of Lake Chelan.

I don't like reservoirs. They are not genuine lakes, not natural. And I have visited the head of Ross "Lake" when no water was in sight, only square miles of stumps and mud, sterilized desolation.

Yet on that promontory a thousand feet above Ross Lake, the drowned valley of the Skagit River, I was impressed. Beautiful. An inland fjord. A fit companion for Lake Chelan. (*If* the lake level is maintained at maximum height during the high-use summer season and *if* the lake level is not raised, as now contemplated, by an addition to Ross Dam.)

Down the final thousand feet to Lightning Creek Camp, our Camp 8, some 26 miles from Castle Pass, 53 miles from Harts Pass. Burt was morose, having half-hoped to be met by his wife bringing a feast of steaks and Guinness. No wife, no steaks, no Guinness. Dehydrated chicken and peas had been delicious before, tasteless now. In the night a bit of sky noise, pit-a-pat on tarp. Low clouds Sunday morning, wind driving waves into the campground, splashing over firepits, lapping at picnic tables, engulfing alders. On the whole trip there couldn't have been a better place or time for crummy weather. Krazy Kat's catamaran from Ross Lake Resort arrived on pre-arranged schedule and carried us downlake 40 miles per hour to Brooks Wives, food, highway, and home.

* * * * *

Thus I learned the country beyond Ross Lake is good for more than Boy Scouts and horses. Still, unregenerate snob, I looked east from the Cascade Crest and wrote off the Pasayten. Once, escaping a monster storm at Harts Pass during the Summer of Fire and Flies, we'd driven the high road from the Methow to the Okanogan and found Tiffany Mountain an oasis of interest. Perhaps a few other scraps of the sort, I judged, but hardly worth a sweat.

A mysterious tussle developed about the North Cascades Bill.

Meadow slopes of Tiffany Mountain; far west, the glacier-white main range of the Cascades.

The legislation omitted from the proposed Pasayten Wilderness Area the far northeast corner of the existing North Cascade Primitive Area. Voices arose from the Okanogan, wailing a protest. Agent Brock investigated and returned raving about Horseshoe Basin. ("No," he had to explain to Puget Sounders, "*Not* the Horseshoe Basin near Cascade Pass. This is *another* Horseshoe Basin—and we must keep it wild!") A last-minute amendment put the corner in the wilderness proposal.

On the Fourth-of-July of 1968 I was seeking an easy highland walk suitable for the Boy (4½) and Eldest Daughter (15), who was recovering from the illness that wiped out her 1967 hiking season. Harts Pass was the first thought, but how about this "other" Horseshoe Basin, anyway? Brock gave details—maybe a shade too enthusiastic to be credible, but worth a gamble. The Brooks-Manning Gang, 10 in all, decided to go see what we were fighting for.

Drive the familiar route by Lake Chelan and up the Columbia, sleeping overnight along the way. But this time pass the Methow and continue to the Okanogan, never before considered an entry to mountains. Drive in hot morning through sagebrush and irrigated orchards to Loomis, in the Sinlahekin valley.

The Sinlahekin: stupendous trench of an Ice Age glacier, wide flat floor meandered by a small and quiet arid-land stream, intense green of irrigation, blistered brown of valley walls. By one definition the Sinlahekin is the eastern boundary of the North Cascades; beyond are Okanogan Highlands, the bridge to the Rockies.

Hot. Temperature in the 90s. Unthinkable for Puget Sounders to walk in such heat. Brock had betrayed us. Drive the road up Toats Coulee Creek. To moldy-skinned, gill-growing citizens of the wet west side, the term, "coulee," suggests dry, dry, barren, death.

Steadily and steeply up from the Sinlahekin. Interesting panoramas, but not for walking. Why had the Forest Service built

From Slate Peak north along the Cascade Crest to Canada; Tamarack Peak in center.

so decent a road? None of the trees (which grow only on high, above the sagebrush) were big enough to be "commercial" by west-side standards.

Drive logging road a mile above sealevel, turn off on a rough track, grinding and wheel-spinning in low gear through shining-white aspen, desert-alpine grasslands, vistas of forested ridges. Betrayed for sure, no pleasant hikes here.

Road-end at Iron Gate Camp, 6000 feet, in a waterless, sun-baking stand of spindly lodgepole pine. Committed now. Had to walk. But didn't want to. While stowing gear in packs, sweating, thirsty, who should greet us but Willis, our man in the Okanogan, one of the guys who set off the chain reaction of events leading to a Congressional reconsideration of Horseshoe Basin. We became instant old friends. For his sake I hoped the country was worth the trouble, but doubted it.

Farewells to Willis, shoulder packs, enter the North Cascade Primitive Area. Hike an abandoned mining road shrunk through the decades to merely a wide trail. A mile of dry, featureless pine, and another, and another. The "good country," if any, must

be close. Small chance it could be very good. A doomed weekend, betrayed.

But in the last ½ mile, a miracle. Climb abruptly into sub-alpine forest, then sky-wide meadows and loud creeks of Sunny Basin, a little glory hole. Score one for Willis and Brock.

Drop packs at Sunny Camp, 6900 feet, run another ½ mile to 7200-foot Sunny Pass, gasp and yell "Hooray!" Vow nevermore to be a snob. Miles of parkland, miles of tundra, rounded, broad summits of 8000-foot peaks. The glaciers that gouged cirques in the primeval hills vanished millenia ago, long before they could sculpt horns and cols; gravity has softened sharp edges cut by ice. A climber could hardly find a pitch requiring use of hands, much less a rope. But a hiker? Infinite wandering in Horseshoe Basin. Is this really the Cascades? More like big-sky gardens of the subarctic.

Singly and in groups, 3 days we roamed, learning. Patches of snow in sheltered nooks, but alpine spring comes to Horseshoe Basin even earlier, almost a month earlier, than Harts Pass. Waterfalls, lakes and ponds, flower fields, green grass.

Climb to tundra plateaus above 8000 feet. Look east to outposts of the Cascades and beyond to Okanogan Highlands. Look north into Canada—and cross the 49th Parallel illegally, visiting monuments erected a half-century ago or more by the International Boundary Commission.

And look west over a lifetime of wild roaming. To the faraway Cascade Crest. On the horizon, dramatic towers and glaciers, incredible volcanoes. Look across the entire range, feel the full dimension east to west. After 20-odd years of studying the Cascades, humbly admit ignorance. The range is larger, more various, than any Puget Sound snob could dream.

The Cascade Crest Trail runs from the Columbia River to Canada, from friendly southern ridges to cold northern crags, passing five volcanoes. Walking time, about a month. Justly famous.

But here's the next plot—to establish a Cross-Cascade Trail.

First week, from Iron Gate to Horseshoe Basin, Scheelite Pass, Cathedral Lakes, Ashnola River, Bunker Hill, Pasayten River. Second week, to the Cascade Crest at Castle Pass, out the Three Fools trail to Ross Lake and around the south end on the lakeshore trail. Third week, through the Pickets via Big Beaver Creek, Beaver Pass, Little Beaver Creek, Whatcom Pass, Brush Creek, Chilliwack River, Hannegan Pass, Ruth Creek. And someday, a fourth week on trails mostly still in imagination, from Shuksan and Baker, beside wild rivers, through new-growing forests, to Puget Sound beaches. That will be a month to remember.

Why stop? Paddle a driftwood raft over saltwater to the Olympic Mountains, cross hills of our long-ago Boy Scout home to surf of the Pacific Ocean. Camp a spell to figure how to handle the next part of the route. Then walk into wildlands forever.

Silver Star Mountain, across the Methow River valley from Mt. Setting Sun.

Snowtime Epilogue

Panorama Dome chairlift, rising from Heather Meadows; in the distance, the Border Peaks.

The North Cascades highland season is short for hikers (including fumble-legged little boys and girls) who can't cope with large quantities of snow. In an average year the far-east meadows of Horseshoe Basin begin to melt free in early June, followed later in the month by the Chelan Crest and Harts Pass and the rainshadow country in general, and near the end of July by the windward country of Glacier Peak, Mt. Baker, and the Pickets.

Sporadic snowfalls resume in September and by November's end or before the winter pile-up — to depths of 20 or 30 feet in some places — is usually underway. In April the snowpack once more starts dwindling toward summer.

So what good to anybody are the North Cascades from November to June, roughly half the year? Some call it the best time of all. The lonely time. The quiet time.

Our Manning Gang sticks mainly to lowlands and front-range hills in deepest winter. Partly because certain members of the group aren't competent to handle snowshoes or skis. Partly because that's our season for surf-watching on wilderness beaches of the Pacific Ocean, in Olympic National Park.

Come late winter and early spring, though, we hunger for

Mt. Baker from Kulshan Ridge.

the North Cascades. Drive, then, up the Cascade River, Suiattle, White Chuck, or Sauk as far as the road is open. A campground crowded in summer is all ours. In the entire valley, only a handful of others come to see forests in mist, or perhaps snow-covered mountains high above in sunshine. Walk a road or trail into snow as far as energy lasts. Tracks of animals. Creeks flowing in white-walled canyons. Avalanches rumbling. Glimpses of peaks chiseled from ice.

Or we may stay below snowline. Voyage up Lake Chelan on the *Lady of the Lake* or *Speedway*, debark at Prince Creek, hike 17½ miles, camping overnight, along the Lakeshore Trail to Stehekin. Or hike from Thunder Arm of Diablo Lake through giant cedars and hemlocks of Thunder Creek. Or the Ross Lakeshore Trail. Or the deep-shadowed arboretum of the Boulder River in the proposed Whitehorse Wilderness Area.

As a family, that's how we enjoy the North Cascades in the quiet time.

For many of our friends the lonely half of the year is the best because it's snowtime. Climbers plug post-holes with boots from April or May on. And through all the winter and spring, skiers and snowshoers hold uncontested ownership of the high valleys and ridges and peaks.

What they own in the quietness and loneliness of snowtime, these photographs suggest.

Snow Crystals and Tree near Austin Pass.

Austin Pass Warming Hut, Table Mountain and Hermans Saddle beyond.

Leaping from a cornice on Shuksan arm
Mt. Baker in distance.

Artist Point and Swift Creek Valley.

Herman Saddle.

Kulshan Ridge and Mount Shuksan.

Colors of the North Cascades

There are days of winter when the peaks are bleached by snow to a single brilliant whiteness. And there are days of summer when steady rain darkens valleys to somber grayness.

But when snow melts away the highlands explode with blossoms, and when the sun emerges forests glow richly green.

And there are sunsets after storms, spectacles beyond sanity. And autumn weeks when all the alpine world is one wild bacchanal.

From forest fungi to sparkling waterfalls to flower gardens to crevasse-slashed glaciers to clouds and sky, the North Cascades are an oratorio of color.

Turn the pages and see.

Sunset on Image Lake and Glacier Peak, the last wild volcano. Unless halted by public opinion, Kennecott Copper Corporation plans to blast an open-pit mine a few minute's walk from the lake.

Lady slipper, a member of the orchid family, beside the Suiattle River trail in the Glacier Peak Wilderness Area.

The Thunder Creek trail, one of the finest forest walks in the North Cascades. However, Seattle City Light is tentatively planning to flood this valley to produce a few more kilowatts.

Skymo Falls on Ross Lake.

South from Slate Peak, the highest point accessible to automobiles in the State of Washington. Harts Pass is hidden by the green ridge. Beyond are unprotected peaks and valleys along the route of the North Cross-State Highway, which should become the North Cascades Parkway.

Glacier Peak from flower fields on Meadow Mountain, above the White Chuck River.

Fireweed in alpine miniature, beside Price Lake, is one of the great holes of Mt. Shuksan.

Highwood Lake, Fall colors, and Mt. Shuksan.

From Sourdough Mountain down to Gorge Lake, a reservoir drowning a portion of the Skagit River.

Sunset from Sahale Arm, above Cascade Pass and the fog-sea of the Cascade River valley; to the left, a bit of Johannesberg Mountain; in the center, Hidden Lake Peaks.

Climber rappelling down Magic Mountain; beyond, Sahale Peak, Boston Mountain, Ripsaw Ridge, and Upper Horseshoe Basin, a headwater of the Stehekin River.

Climbers on a pinnacle above the Honeycomb Glacier; beyond, winter-white Glacier Peak.

Left: Crevasse on the Challenger Glacier.

Right: The rock-block summit tower of Mt. Challenger and the broad sweep of the Challenger Glacier, from a snowmelt pool on the flanks of Challenger Ridge.

Following page: Aspen in Fall, beside the road from Sinlahekin valley (east boundary of the Cascades) to the Pasayten Wilderness Area.

A Portfolio of the North Cascades

Snowfield Peak and the Neve Glacier.

Yellow violet.

Bridge over Thunder Creek.

Begin on beaches of Puget Sound. Walk through second-growth trees and moss and ferns, beside free-running rivers, from lowlands into foothills. Enter virgin forests, shadowed canyons, the streams brawling loud. Follow steepening valleys, the trees growing shorter, the water whiter. Suddenly break into flowers and wide sky. Up meadows, up moraines, up snowfields. Climb glaciers and rocks to a summit with far horizons.

Someday there must be such a trail, a re-creation of the frontier wilderness partly destroyed, partly still saved. People are at work now in the State of Washington to make the walk possible, to let hikers learn the North Cascades from bottom to top.

From bottom to top: not the "Alpine" way, starting the acquaintance above any rivers worth polluting or drowning, any trees worth chopping, any flowers worth eating, any rocks worth gouging.

Moraines and glaciers and cliffs are superb, but the way to know mountains to the full is the wild way of the North Cascades, from far down in luxuriant greenery to far up in the sky.

This portfolio shows the way from low to high, which in the North Cascades are all one, a single wilderness world.

Trillium.

Nurse log, hemlock, ferns, moss.

Ferns and falls.

*Man and dog crossing the trail bridge over the Suiattle River, in
springtime evening, to enter the Glacier Peak Wilderness Area.*

Deadly amanita.

Puffballs.

Miners Ridge lookout, the Suiattle River valley, and Glacier Peak.

Looking over the fog-filled Methow River valley from Mt. Setting Sun.

Marble Creek, where beaver thrive. Around the corner
is Eldorado Peak.

Vanilla leaf ("sweet after death") with rain drops and sunshine.

Canadian dogwood, or bunchberry.

Fog in Swift Creek, cloudcap on Mt. Baker, sunset light on higher clouds.

Twin Lakes, Nooksack River valley, and Mt. Baker.

On the trail from Twin Lakes to Winchester Peak lookout.

On Sourdough Mountain, Thunder Arm of Diablo Lake below. In center horizon is the head of Thunder Creek at Park Creek Pass, flanked left by Mt. Logan and right by Mt. Buckner and the Boston Glacier.

Tour boat on Diablo Lake, a drowned section of the Skagit River; beyond, Paul Bunyan's Stump (What's the Matterhorn) and Pyramid Peak.

Air view above Sauk River valley; White Chuck Peak, left, and Mt. Pugh, right center, face each other across the White Chuck River.

From Sahale Arm, above Cascade Pass, to Magic Mountain.

Whatcom Peak from Challenger Ridge.

Kool Ade Lake, a favorite campsite on the Ptarmigan Traverse; Mt. Formidable beyond.

Suiattle River forests from the Green Mountain logging road. Ultimately, unless the people force another decision, the Forest Service will build many more such roads in this valley and cut all these trees, patch by patch.

The un-named glacier in Boston Basin; above, Sahale Peak.

Crevasses on Mt. Baker.

Iceberg Lake; above, Hermans Saddle and cliffs of Table Mountain.

The Roosevelt and Coleman Glaciers and the Black Buttes, from
Bastille Ridge on Mt. Baker.

The South Cascade Glacier. To the left, Old Guard and Sentinel Peaks. In the background, Gunsight (Blue), Sinister, and Dome Peaks. The U.S. Geological Survey research hut is on the rock rib beside the glacier.

A new lake at the foot of the Perfect Glacier (also known as the north segment of the Challenger Glacier). In 1950 the ice extended well beyond this point, the lake-to-be foreshadowed by a sink hole in the glacier surface.

126

From Sentinel Peak across the West Fork of Agnes Creek to Sinister and Dome Peaks and the Chickamin and Dana Glaciers; on the horizon, Glacier Peak.

The Needle, above the Ladder Creek tongue of the Neve Glacier.

Climbers on Mt. Shuksan. They've just emerged from the Fischer
Chimneys and are approaching the base of Winnie's Slide.

Crevasse on Mt. Challenger.

On the un-named glacier in Boston Basin.

Climbing the Challenger Glacier toward the summit of Mt. Challenger,
still some 500 feet above.

On the Coleman Glacier of Mt. Baker.

Air view of the McMillan Cirque wall of the Southern Pickets; Inspiration Peak left, The Pyramid and Degenhardt Peak in center, Mt. Terror just out of the picture to right.

Air view of Mt. Shuksan from the north; Nooksack Tower on left ridge, the Price Glacier in center, Mt. Baker beyond to the right.

Boulder hopping on Magic Mountain.

Climbers descending Mt. Shuksan, getting nerved up to go over the brink of Winnie's Slide, the uppermost part of the White Salmon Glacier.

Summit rocks of Magic Mountain;
Eldorado Peak in clouds to the left.

High on Mt. Challenger. Left of Whatcom Peak are cornice-edged Perfect Pass and the long arc of Easy Ridge; right, out of sight, is Whatcom Pass. The wide gulf of Chilliwack River runs from left to right. Beyond, on the horizon left of center, are Mt. Tomyhoi and the Border Peaks; facing them across the valley of Silesia Creek is the tower of Slesse Peak, just over the border in Canada.

Snowfield Peak and the Neve Glacier.